THE NEW LEADER'S 100-DAY ACTION PLAN

THE NEW LEADER'S 100-DAY ACTION PLAN

FOURTH EDITION

HOW TO **TAKE CHARGE, BUILD** OR **MERGE YOUR TEAM,** AND **GET IMMEDIATE RESULTS**

GEORGE B. BRADT | JAYME A. CHECK | JOHN A. LAWLER

WILEY

Library of Congress Cataloging-in-Publication Data:

Names: Bradt, George B. | Check, Jayme A. | Lawler, John A.
Title: The new leader's 100-day action plan: how to take charge, build or merge your team, and get immediate results/George B. Bradt, Jayme A. Check, John A. Lawler.
Description: 4th Edition. | Hoboken: Wiley, 2016. | Revised edtion of The new leader's 100-day action plan, 2011. | Includes bibliographical references and index.
Identifiers: LCCN 2015038533 | ISBN 9781119223238 (cloth)
Subjects: LCSH: Leadership—Handbooks, manuals, etc.
Classification: LCC HD57.7 .B723 2016 | DDC 658.4/092—dc23 LC record available at http://lccn.loc.gov/2015038533

CONTENTS

Wﾠe did not write this book as much as discover it. To a large degree, it is the product of all the transitions that have influenced all the people who have ever influenced us. Throughout our careers, we have learned by doing, by watching, and by interacting with a whole range of leaders—bosses, coaches, peers, subordinates, partners, and clients. We end every PrimeGenesis interaction with two questions: What was particularly valuable? How can we make it even more valuable? It is amazing what you can learn by asking.

What you have in your hands was born of continuing to ask those questions and the realization that onboarding is a crucible of leadership. Done poorly, it results in a lot of pain for a lot of people. Done well, the benefits are amazing, positively transforming leaders, organizations, and teams.

We would need a separate book to credit all the people who have had the most positive influence on us over the years. But we must acknowledge the contributions of our past and current partners at PrimeGenesis. Their fingerprints are all over this book as we all work these ideas every day.

In particular, we thank Jorge Pedraza, who was one of the founding partners of PrimeGenesis and one of the original coauthors of this book through its first, second, and third editions. Aside from being a brilliant thought leader and team leader, Jorge is easily the best author among us. So if you're reading a passage in this book that seems particularly well written, Jorge probably originally crafted it.

We are indebted to the clients of PrimeGenesis on several levels. We are the first to admit that we have learned more from them than they have from us. We give our clients complete confidentiality, so we have masked individuals' and companies' names in the stories involving any of our clients. We are blessed to have the opportunity to work with an extremely diverse group of clients. They run the gamut from the multinational to the small, from public company to private, from for-profit to not-for-profit. The executives we work with come from many industries, from almost every discipline imaginable, and from many parts of the world. With every client, we have learned something new. Clients inspire, challenge, and teach us on a daily basis, and for that we are grateful. You can learn more about our list of clients on our website at www.PrimeGenesis.com.

We also thank the readers around the world whose enthusiastic embrace of the ideas in this book has kept us motivated to keep it current. We have the good fortune of truly engaged readers who download tools and interact with us on a daily basis from around the globe. We thank you for buying the book, passing it on, and reaching out to us to share your ideas, praise, constructive criticism, successes, and truly insightful questions.

Abounding gratitude to George's editor at *Forbes*, Fred Allen, and our editor at John Wiley & Sons, Richard Narramore. Each of them has nurtured our ideas and gently pushed us to make them better across the years.

And, finally, to our families and loved ones. We deeply appreciate your unending encouragement and support along the way.

Are you a veteran chief executive officer (CEO) taking the reins of your next organization? Starting a new role as a frontline supervisor? Something in between? Whether you are joining a new organization from the outside, getting promoted from within, leading a reorganization or restart, or merging teams following an acquisition, *The New Leader's 100-Day Action Plan* will help you take charge, build your team, set direction, and deliver better results faster than anyone thought possible.

> *We've found that 40 percent of executives hired at the senior level are pushed out, fail or quit within 18 months. It's expensive in terms of lost revenue. It's expensive in terms of the individual's hiring. It's damaging to morale.*
>
> —Kevin Kelly, CEO of executive search firm
> Heidrick & Struggles, discussing the firm's
> internal study of 20,000 searches.[1]

What do these failed leaders not see, know, do, or deliver? In most cases, they dig their own holes by missing one or more crucial tasks in their first 100 days. Some don't understand the impact of their early words and actions and inadvertently send their new colleagues the wrong messages. Some focus on finding a new strategy, but fail to get buy-in and build trust with their new team. Some expend a lot of energy on the wrong projects without accomplishing the one or two things that their most important stakeholders expected them to deliver.

All are unaware of some of the important steps required to achieve a successful transition. No new leader wants to fail, but it happens at an alarming rate.

Meanwhile, if you're working at or owned by a private equity firm, the pressures can be even more intense. Gone are the days of delivering

---

[1] Quoted in Brooke Masters, 2009, "Rise of a Headhunter," *Financial Times*, March 30.

returns through debt and multiple arbitrage. Assets are fully priced, reflecting information transparency, surplus investment capital, and competitive buying environments. To deliver competitive returns, you must create meaningful value through organic improvements in operations and integration of accretive acquisitions over relatively short time frames. See Figure 0.1 below.

Whether you are operating in a major corporation, a smaller start-up, or a midsized business, delivering value is not getting any easier, particularly in complex situations where transformation and speed are musts. Failure rates are high—83 percent of acquisitions fail to produce expected returns,[2] and only 26 percent of transformations are deemed very or completely successful.[3]

This won't happen to you. Not if you let us help you.

Let's start at the beginning.

Our fundamental, underlying concept is that onboarding is a crucible of leadership and that:

> Leadership is about inspiring and enabling others to do their absolute best together to realize a meaningful and rewarding shared purpose.

FIGURE 0.1   Value Buildup in Private Equity (Notional Example) in Billions of Dollars

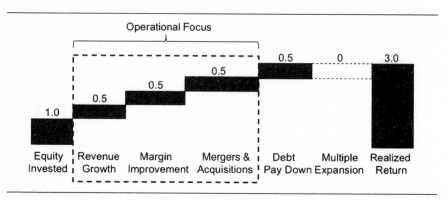

Source: Capital Roundtable Conference, September 2014.

---

[2] KPMG study, reported by Margaret Heffernan, 2012, "Why Mergers Fail," CBS Money Watch, April 24.

[3] Study by Rajiv Chandran, Hortense de la Boutetier, and Carolyn Dewar, 2015, "Ascending to the C-Suite," McKinsey Insights, April.

It's not about you. It's not even about those following you. It's about the shared purpose, the cause, and what you and they hear, see, believe, feel, and accomplish together as a team. Leadership is about your ability to create a culture in which your team can deliver remarkable results and love doing it. Effective leadership occurs when a team's behaviors, relationships, attitudes, values, and environment are synchronized to achieve the best results possible.

The Chinese philosopher Lao-tzu expressed this particularly well more than 2,500 years ago:

> "The great leader speaks little. He never speaks carelessly. He works without self-interest and leaves no trace. When all is finished, the people say, 'We did it ourselves.'"[4]

With that in mind, this is a practical playbook complete with the tools, action plans, timelines, and key milestones you need to reach along the way to accelerate your own and your team's success in your first 100 days and beyond.

Our insights are gleaned from our own leadership experiences and from the work of our firm, PrimeGenesis, whose sole mission is to help executives and teams deliver better results faster during complex transitions. Across all of our clients, the 100-Day Action Plan approach has reduced the failure rate for new leaders from the industry average of 40 percent to less than 5 percent. Our top 10 onboarding clients have deployed us more than 140 times.

Since 2003, leaders and teams in public multinationals, such as American Express and Johnson & Johnson; in midsize entities owned by private equity firms, such as MacAndrews & Forbes and Clayton, Dubilier & Rice; and in not-for-profit organizations, such as the Red Cross, have implemented the 100-Day Action Plan. They have deployed it across a wide range of functions and complex transitions, including executive onboarding, turnarounds, start-ups, reorganizations, and merging leadership teams during acquisitions.

The core principles and techniques we deploy to make our impact on senior leaders and teams are described in this book. *The New Leader's 100-Day Action Plan* is the same plan we help executives develop and deliver in work with clients. The tools work for leaders transitioning into new roles or merging teams at any level, in any environment.

---

[4] Paraphrasing the seventeenth verse of the *Tao Te Ching* by Lao-Tzu.

Over the years, we have noticed that many new leaders show up for a new role happy and smiling but without a plan. Neither they, nor their organizations, have thought things through in advance. On their first day, they are welcomed by such confidence-building remarks as: "Oh, you're here . . . we'd better find you an office."

Ouch!

Some enlightened organizations have a better process in place. They put people in charge of preparing for leaders' transitions. Imagine the difference when a new leader is escorted to an office that is fully set up for him or her, complete with computer, passwords, phones, files, information, and a 30-day schedule of orientation and assimilation meetings.

Better . . . but still not good enough.

Even if the company has set everything up for you, if you have waited until your first day on the job to start, you are already behind with the odds stacked against you. Paradoxically, the best way to accelerate a complex pivot like going into a new role is to pause long enough to think through a plan before you start, put it in place early, and then get a head start on implementing it.

As the leader, you must align all stakeholders around a shared purpose and set of objectives, set a compelling direction, build a cohesive leadership team, and create a culture that enables excellent execution.

As it turns out, these are some of the most difficult tasks faced by leaders entering complex situations, made even more challenging when compounded by the need for speed.

Having a process and set of tools can help you use your first 100 days to meet these challenges and propel you down the path to success.

The four main ideas are:

1. **Get a head start.** Day One is a critical pivot point for people moving into new roles or merging teams. In both situations, you can accelerate progress by getting a head start and hitting the ground running. Preparation in the days and weeks leading up to Day One breeds confidence; and a little early momentum goes a long way.

2. **Manage the message.** Everything communicates. People read things into everything you say and do and everything you don't say and don't do. You're far better off choosing and guiding what others see and hear, and when they see and hear it, rather than letting happenstance or others make those choices for you. Start

this process with your current best thinking before Day One and adjust steadfastly as you go along.

3. **Set direction. Build the team.** The first 100 days is the best time to put in place the basic building blocks of a cohesive, high-performing team. You will fail if you try to create the organization's imperative yourself, without the support and buy-in of your team. As a team leader, your own success is inextricably linked to the success of the team as a whole.

4. **Sustain momentum. Deliver results.** Although the first 100 days are a sprint to jump-start communication, team building, and core practices, it's all for naught if you then sit back and watch things happen. You must evolve your leadership, practices, and culture to keep fueling the fires you sparked and deliver ongoing results.

These four ideas are built on the frameworks of highly effective teams and organizations and flow through the book (see Figure 0.2). It's helpful to explain them up front. First, the headlines:

High-performing teams and organizations are built of people, plans, and practices aligned around a shared purpose.

Tactical capacity bridges the gap between strategy and execution, ensuring that a good strategy doesn't fail because of bad execution.

Six building blocks underpin a team's tactical capacity: communication, Burning Imperative, milestones, early wins, roles, and then ongoing evolution.

FIGURE 0.2   Core Frameworks

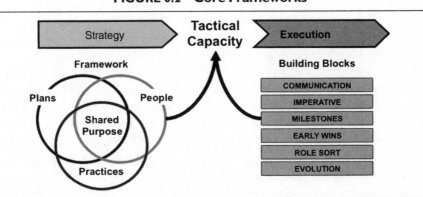

People-Plans-Practices

An organization's or team's performance is based on aligning its people, plans, and practices around a shared purpose. This involves getting strong *people* in the right roles with the right support, clarity around the strategies and action steps included in *plans*, and *practices* in place that enable people to work together in a systematic and effective way. The heart of this is a clearly understood, meaningful, and rewarding *shared purpose*.

Tactical Capacity

Tactical capacity is a team's ability to work under difficult, changing conditions and to translate strategies into tactical actions decisively, rapidly, and effectively. It is the essential bridge between strategy and execution.

In contrast with other work groups that move slowly, with lots of direction and most decision making coming from the leader, high-performing teams with strong tactical capacity empower each member, communicating effectively with the team and the leader (you), to come up with critical solutions to the inevitable problems that arise on an ongoing basis and to implement them quickly.

The objective is high-quality responsiveness; it takes cohesive teamwork to make it happen. High-performing teams build on strategy and plans with strong people and practices to implement ever-evolving and acutely responsive actions that work.

> *It is not the strongest of the species that survives, nor the most intelligent, but the one most responsive to change.*

—Attributed to Charles Darwin

You probably have seen this yourself. You may have been on teams with members who operate in disconnected silos, incapable of acting without specific direction from above. They may know the strategy. They may have the resources they need, but any variation or change paralyzes them. The Federal Emergency Management Agency (FEMA) actually had run the drill on a major hurricane in New Orleans months before Katrina hit. But the plan collapsed with the first puff of wind because no one could react flexibly and insightfully to a situation that was different from what FEMA had expected.

In contrast, a great example of tactical capacity at work was the way the National Aeronautics and Space Administration (NASA) team members came together during the Apollo 13 crisis. Right from "Houston, we've had a problem," the team reacted flexibly and fluidly to a dramatic and unwelcome new reality—a crippling explosion en route, in space.

The team went beyond its standard operating procedures and what its equipment was "designed to do" to exploring what it "could do." Through tight, on-the-fly collaboration, the team did in minutes what normally took hours, in hours what normally took days, and in days what normally took months. This teamwork was critical to getting the crew home safely.

If you're lucky, you've been on teams where actions and results flow with great ease, where team members know what is really required and intended and support each other in making those things happen. Those teams have tactical capacity.

As the new leader, it's your job to orchestrate the alignment of people, plans, and practices around a shared purpose—and then build tactical capacity to ensure excellent execution. You must help key people co-create a Burning Imperative and deliver against it with a great sense of urgency. A Burning Imperative created this way is the antidote to silos and departments that don't cooperate. Tactical capacity is not only about the team responding quickly to changes in external circumstances, but it also is about team members working well with each other in support of the team's Burning Imperative.

Building Blocks of Tactical Capacity

The good news is that, as a leader in a new role, you can build tactical capacity into your team quickly by implementing six building blocks:

1. Drive culture and action with ongoing communication.
2. Embed a strong Burning Imperative.
3. Exploit key milestones to drive team performance.
4. Overinvest in early wins to build team confidence.
5. Secure the right people in the right roles with the right support.
6. Evolve your leadership, practices, and culture to deliver results continually.

The NASA team dealing with the Apollo 13 got each of these six building blocks in place, allowing it to react with tactical capacity of the highest order:

1. The culture had been strong. But everyone's communication reinforced the message that "failure is not an option" throughout the rescue mission.

2. The team's mission changed from "go to the moon to collect rocks" to the one Burning Imperative of "get these men home alive." This was galvanizing enough (as a Burning Imperative must always be) to transcend all petty issues and focus everyone's efforts.

3. The team's milestones were clear: Turn the ship around, preserve enough energy to allow a reentry, fix the carbon monoxide problem, survive the earth's atmosphere, and so on.

4. The carbon monoxide fix allowed the astronauts to stay alive and was the early win that made the team believe it could do the rest of the things that would get the crew back to Earth safely. It gave everyone confidence.

5. Everyone was working with the same end in mind but working in different and essential roles. One group figured out how to turn the spaceship around. Another group fixed the oxygen problem. Another dealt with the reentry calculations, and the spare crew did whatever it took to complete the mission.

6. Once the immediate issue and Burning Imperative had been resolved, NASA embedded rigorous practices to minimize risks and maximize performance as standard operating procedure going forward.

Even though you're unlikely to jump into a situation exactly like the Apollo 13 breakdown, in today's environment almost all leadership transitions are "hot landings," where you must hit the ground running to have a chance of success.

Often you will need to fix something, maybe a few things, fast. Sometimes you will have more time to plan. In most onboarding situations, you will have at least a few days to create an onboarding plan—especially if you give yourself a head start. Time is like air (without carbon monoxide!) to breathe, and a head start gives you time. Your first plan gets you moving in the right direction; it will evolve as you learn more and things change—which they will.

The 100-Day Action Plan

Here are the steps in the onboarding process—and the chapters in this book:

Get a Head Start

1. Position yourself for success: Get the job. Make sure it is right for you. Avoid common landmines.

2. Leverage the Fuzzy Front End: Jump-start relationships. Listen, learn, and plan before Day One.

Manage the Message

3. Take control of Day One: Make a powerful first impression. Confirm your entry message.

4. Activate ongoing communication: Establish leadership and begin cultural transformation.

Set Direction. Build the Team

5. Pivot to strategy: Co-create the Burning Imperative by Day 30.

6. Drive operational accountability: Embed milestones by Day 45 and early wins by Day 60.

7. Strengthen the organization: Get the right team in place by Day 70.

Sustain Momentum. Deliver Results

8. Keep building: Evolve your leadership, practices, and culture to deliver results.

Figure 0.3 lays out the steps of the onboarding process, the 100-Day Action Plan.

Culture

In many respects, leadership is an exercise in building culture. However you define it, culture is the glue that holds organizations together. It may be the only truly sustainable competitive advantage[5] and the root cause of every merger's success or failure.[6] This book focuses on pivotal events, such as joining a new organization or merging teams, as opportunities to accelerate culture change and results. They are about creating and bridging gaps: gaps between a leader and his or her new team, gaps between an aspirational state and the current reality.

You must consider culture throughout your 100-Day Plan. Especially when you:

- Prepare for interviews (to answer cultural fit questions)
- Complete your due diligence (to mitigate organizational, role, and personal land mines)
- Choose your onboarding approach (by comparing the business' need for change to the culture's readiness for change)
- Converge into the organizational culture
- Evolve the organization's culture

Cultural elements are particularly critical to get right in a post-merger integration. Too little effort is paid to culture during integrations, 70 percent of those surveyed in the 2009 Post Merger Integration Conference acknowledged, with 92 percent claiming that greater cultural understanding would have substantially benefited mergers in their experience. And, respondents assigned blame for cultural difficulties to "poor leadership of the integration effort" as opposed to "wrong choice of target" by a factor of five to one![7] The message: Culture is critical, and leadership matters.

Keep culture a crucial consideration in everything you do. To help, you can find all the thoughts and tools on culture in this book pulled together in one document at www.onboardingtools.com (Tool 1A.10).

---

[5] George Bradt, 2012, "Corporate Culture: The Only Truly Sustainable Competitive Advantage," *Forbes*, February 8.
[6] George Bradt, 2015, "The Root Cause of Every Merger's Success or Failure: Culture," *Forbes*, June 29.
[7] Clay Deutsch and Andy West, 2010, *Perspectives on Merger Integration*, McKinsey, June.

Communication—It Starts with Listening

The other thread that runs through the book is communication. Because everything communicates, guidance on communication belongs in every step and every chapter.

One idea that jars some people is the recommendation to craft your going-in message before Day One. Leaders wonder how they can do that before they've completed their listening tour. You will have learned a fair amount about the organization, its priorities, and its people during your interview and due diligence stages. If you know enough to have been offered and accepted the job, you know enough to craft an initial going-in message so that you can take control of your own entry. Take your current best thinking, craft a hypothetical message, and use that to direct your future learning.

Chapter 1: Position Yourself for Success: Get the Job. Make Sure it is Right for You. Avoid Common Land Mines

Leadership is personal. Your message is the key that unlocks personal connections. The greater the congruence between your own preferences across behaviors, relationships, attitudes, values, and environment and the new culture you enter or create, the stronger those connections and your message will be. This is why the best messages aren't crafted—they emerge. This is why great leaders live their messages not because they can, but because they must. "Here I stand, I can do no other."[8]

Knowing your own strengths and cultural preferences will help you better create career options that are a true fit for you, will allow you to do a better job positioning yourself in interviews (selling before you buy), and will help you do a thorough due diligence to mitigate risks.

Chapter 2: Leverage the Fuzzy Front End: Jump-Start Relationships. Listen, Learn, and Plan Before Day One

At this point you've made the choice—but you haven't started yet. There's a temptation to take a deep breath and relax. Don't do that.

---

[8] Attributed to Martin Luther at the Diet of Worms, 1521, when asked to recant his earlier writings.

What you do next, what you do before Day One, can make all the difference. So, choose the right approach for your situation, draft a plan, and get a head start.

There are a couple of dimensions to choosing the right approach. First, the approach is different if you're joining a new company, getting promoted or transferred from within, running a private equity–owned business, crossing international boundaries, or merging teams. Second, the business context and the culture's readiness for change will inform your choice around whether to assimilate in slowly, converge and evolve, or shock the organization with sudden changes.

Armed with the choice about your overall approach, you're ready to create a 100-day plan targeting the most important stakeholders up, across, and down—both inside the organization and out, laying out your best current thinking around your message, what you're going to do between now and Day One, on Day One, and over your first 100 days and beyond. These efforts include prestart conversations to jump-start your important relationships and learning, as well as focus on various aspects of your personal setup.

These steps are especially critical in merging or restarting teams where no one will focus on the strategy or team until they know what their own personal role and responsibilities will be in the new order. Thus, two important steps in a merger or acquisition are to (1) complete an initial role sort (possibly even before the deal closes) so that you are able to inform all team members of their new roles and (2) enroll the leadership team in the change process, starting with co-creating the combined team's initial change messages.

MasterCard's Ajay Banga managed his Fuzzy Front End and early days particularly well. He leveraged the time after he had been announced as CEO but before he started by casually, but pointedly, interacting with key stakeholders with a simple introduction: "Hi, I'm Ajay. Tell me about yourself."[9]

---

[9] George Bradt, 2011, "Why Preparing in Advance Is Priceless: How MasterCard CEO Ajay Banga Planned Ahead for His New Leadership Role," *Forbes*, February 23.

Chapter 3: Take Control of Day One: Make a Powerful First Impression. Confirm Your Entry Message

Everything is magnified on Day One, whether you are joining a new company, entering a private equity portfolio, or announcing an acquisition. Everyone is looking for hints about what you think and what you're going to do. People's only real question is "What does this mean for me?"

This is why it's so important to seed your message by paying particular attention to all the signs, symbols, and stories you deploy, and the order in which you deploy them. Make sure that people are seeing and hearing things that will lead them to believe and feel what you want them to believe and feel about you and about themselves in relation to the future of the organization.

The Sierra Club's executive director Michael Brune did a particularly good job of managing his Day One. He thought through his message in advance and then communicated it live, face-to-face, and via social media on his first day so that everyone would know what was on his mind. He smartly used several communication methods to reach a wide range of people in their own preferred way of communication.[10]

Chapter 4: Activate Ongoing Communication: Establish Leadership and Begin Cultural Transformation

The prescription for communication during the time between Day One and co-creating a Burning Imperative is counterintuitive and stressful for new leaders following this program. The fundamental approach is to converge and evolve. And the time before co-creating a Burning Imperative is all about converging. This means you can't launch your full-blown communication efforts yet. You can't stand up and tell people your new ideas. If you do, they are your ideas, not invented here and not the team's ideas.

---

[10] George Bradt, 2011, "Powerful First Impressions: Michael Brune's Day One at the Sierra Club," *Forbes*, March 2.

So at this point, refine your current best thinking about communication, and begin to establish your leadership and transform the culture by your questions, your active listening, and your behaviors, not by what you say.

Chapter 5: Pivot to Strategy: Co-Create the Burning Imperative by Day 30

The Burning Imperative is a sharply defined, intensely shared, and purposefully urgent understanding from the team members of what they are "supposed to do, now," and how this works with the larger aspirations of the team and the organization.

Although mission, vision, and values are often components of the Burning Imperative, the critical piece is the rallying cry that everyone understands and can act on. Co-create this with the team to get buy-in early, even if your best current thinking is only 90 percent right. You, and your team, will adjust and improve along the way. Don't let anything distract you from getting this in place and shared—in your first 30 days!

Chapter 6: Drive Operational Accountability: Embed Milestones by Day 45 and Early Wins by Day 60

The real test of a high-performing team's tactical capacity lies in the formal and informal practices that are at work across team members, particularly around clarifying decision rights and information flows.[11]

The core responsibility of a high-performing team's leader is to inspire and enable others to do their absolute best, together. These leaders spend more time integrating across than managing down. The milestone tool is straightforward and focuses on mapping and tracking who is doing what, by when. High-performing team leaders take that basic tool to a whole new level, exploiting it to inspire and enable people to work together as a team!

---

[11] Gary L. Neilson, Karla L. Martin, and Elizabeth Powers, 2008, "The Secrets to Successful Strategy Execution," *Harvard Business Review*, June.

Royal Caribbean's CEO Richard Fain explains it this way:

If you don't establish early on key milestones—long-term milestones rather than the short-term milestones—you get caught in the "next week" syndrome. . . . Everybody says, "We're going to know so much more next week or the week after" . . . so the focus shifts to next week or the week after and we all desperately wait for that period. Meanwhile the longer-term milestone goes by the wayside.[12]

Early wins are all about credibility and confidence. People have more faith in people who have delivered. You want team members to have confidence in you, in themselves, and in the plan for change that has emerged. You want your boss to have confidence in you. Early wins fuel that confidence. To that end, jump-start potential early wins by Day 60, and overinvest to deliver them by the end of your first six months—as a team!

Chapter 7: Strengthen the Organization: Get the Right Team in Place by Day 70

Make your organization stronger by acquiring, developing, encouraging, planning, and transitioning talent:

Acquire: Recruit, attract, and onboard the right people.

Develop: Assess and build skills and knowledge.

Encourage: Direct, support, recognize, and reward.

Plan: Monitor, assess, and plan career moves over time.

Transition: Migrate to different roles as appropriate.

Start by defining the right structure and roles to execute on your mission. Be specific about requirements for success in each key role, and then match them with the right talent.

Pay attention to differences. The world needs three types of leaders: scientific leaders who influence knowledge, artistic leaders who influence feelings, and interpersonal leaders who influence actions. These three are not always mutually exclusive. Jump-start your team by getting the right people in the right roles with the right support to build the team.

---

[12] George Bradt, 2011, "Royal Caribbean's CEO Exemplifies How to Leverage Milestones," *Forbes*, March 23.

Chapter 8: Keep Building: Evolve Your Leadership, Practices and Culture to Deliver Results

By the 100-day mark you will have put a plan in place, leveraged the time before Day One to learn quickly, developed solid relationships with key stakeholders, engaged the culture, and made a strong early impression by delivering a clear message to your new audiences (up, down, and across). Your team will be in place, energized by its co-created Burning Imperative, and will have established milestone management practices to drive accountability and have early wins in sight.

So, what's next? Begin the process of continual evolution in three key areas:

1. **Leadership:** The 100-day mark is a good moment to gain feedback on your own leadership during the first 100 days so that you can determine *what* you should keep, stop, and start doing—and *how*—to be even more effective with your team and the organization as a whole.

2. **Practices:** From there, it is an opportune time to decide how you are going to evolve your practices to capitalize on changing circumstances. You should focus on practices that relate to people, plans, performance tracking, and program management.

3. **Culture:** Finally, after 100 days, your insights on the culture will be sharper than when you started. Also, you will be clearer about how you want to *evolve the culture*. Now is the time to zero in on the biggest gaps and implement a plan to create and maintain the winning culture that will become your greatest competitive advantage.

By evolving your own leadership, practices, and culture, you will be setting yourself and your team up to deliver better results faster and sustainably over time.

Walmart's CEO Mike Duke knows that we are all new leaders all the time. That's why organizational change management is an ongoing part of his life. When Walmart's merchandising failed to deliver the expected results over the 2010 holiday season, Mike replaced his head merchandiser and completely revamped their holiday merchandising approach in time to be able to announce the changes in their next quarter's earnings call.[13]

---

[13] George Bradt, 2011, "Walmart CEO Mike Duke Shifts Approach," *Forbes*, March 1.

Make This Book Work for You

By now you should be aware that there may be a better way to manage transitions than just showing up on Day One or charging into your promotion announcement or newly merged team and doing what *they* tell you to do. Similarly, there may be a better way for you to tackle this book than just starting on page one and reading straight through until you lose steam.

This is designed to be a flexible playbook split into three parts: (1) the book itself, (2) downloadable and editable tools, and (3) more extensive notes and content on www.onboardingtools.com. You might want to start with the 100-Day worksheet (Tool 2.1) at the end of Chapter 2 or the sample 100-day worksheets on the website. You might prefer to begin with the chapter summaries or to read straight through the main body of the book. Use the book's elements in the way that works best for you.

People often tell us, "This is just common sense. But I like the way you've structured it." (One person said, "You brought together all of the critical thinking sessions I had with myself in the shower every morning before work!" We'll let you imagine that in your own way.)

Do be aware of our bias to push you to do things faster than others would expect. The 100-Day Plan is based on the needs of new leaders moving into complex situations who must meet or beat high expectations fast, but it may not be appropriate for your situation without some customization. We present you options and choices. You are in charge. We wish you success in your new leadership role. We hope this book will help you and your team deliver better results faster than anyone thought possible!

Position Yourself for Success

GET THE JOB. MAKE SURE IT IS RIGHT FOR YOU. AVOID COMMON LAND MINES.

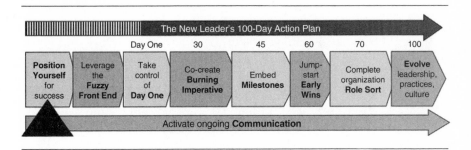

As discussed in the executive summary, the four main ideas in this book are: (1) Get a head start; (2) Manage the message; (3) Set direction. Build the team; (4) Sustain momentum. Deliver results.

As you start to position yourself for success, know that leadership is personal. Your message is the key that unlocks personal connections. The greater the congruence between your own preferences across behaviors, relationships, attitudes, values, and environment and the new culture you enter or create, the stronger those connections will be. This is why the best messages aren't crafted—they emerge. This is why great leaders live their messages not because they can, but because they must. "Here I stand, I can do no other."[1]

Knowing your strengths and motivations will help you better create career options that are a true fit for your skills, will allow you to better position yourself in interviews (sell before you buy), and will help you do a thorough due diligence to mitigate risks.

"I wish I'd read this chapter before I accepted that job!"

We hear that a lot.

Culture First

In many respects, leadership is an exercise in building culture. However you define it, culture is the glue that holds organizations together. It may be the only truly sustainable competitive advantage for any organization. Culture is often impacted by pivotal events, such as a new leader joining an organization, presenting opportunities to accelerate culture change and deliver better results. Culture change is about bridging the gap between the current state and the desired state—that which is needed to achieve the organization's mission and goals.

The greater the cultural differences, the more difficult the adaptation or change will be. There's real power in understanding the most important cultural differences and then building a plan to bridge those gaps over time.

Some define culture simply as "the way we do things around here." Others conduct complex analyses to define it more scientifically. Instead, blend both schools of thought into an implementable approach that defines culture as an organization's behaviors, relationships, attitudes, values, and the environment (BRAVE). The BRAVE framework is relatively easy to apply yet offers a relatively robust way to identify, engage, and change a culture. It makes culture real, tangible, identifiable, and easy to talk about.

It's helpful to tackle the BRAVE components from the outside in with five questions, as shown in Table 1.1.

When evaluating each element of culture, think of it on a sliding scale (say 1–5), rather than in absolute terms. The specific dimensions within each cultural component may vary from situation to situation.

---

[1] Attributed to Martin Luther at the Diet of Worms, 1521, when asked to recant his earlier writings.

Table 1.1
BRAVE Framework

Environment	Where to play?	(Context)
Values	What matters and why?	(Purpose)
Attitudes	How to win?	(Choices)
Relationships	How to connect?	(Communication)
Behaviors	What impact?	(Implementation)

You may find the components and dimensions below particularly useful.

Environment is where the organization decides to play in the context of the situation it faces. Consider:

- Is the impetus for growth found more in opportunities to capture or more in problems to solve?
- Are the growth enablers more human, interpersonal, and societal or more technological, mechanical, and scientific?
- Are the main barriers more external hurdles or more internal capabilities?

Values are what matters to the organization and its people and why. Consider:

- What's the organization's purpose: mission (why), vision (what), and values (how), and is it interpreted more as intended and evolving or more as written and set?
- Is the approach to risk more about risking more to gain more over time or more about protecting what is now?
- Is the approach to learning more open and shared or more directed?

Attitudes are how the organization chooses to win across strategy, posture, and approach. Consider:

- Is the fundamental strategy more premium price, innovation, and high service or more low price, minimum viable product, and self-service?

- Is there a bias more toward creating ideas and pushing them out to the market or more toward doing things in response to customers' needs?
- Do people strive to be more proactive or more responsive?

Relationships are about how the organization connects. Consider:

- Are power and decision making more diffused and debated or more controlled to the point of being monarchical?
- Do people communicate more informally, verbally and face-to-face, or more formally, directed and written?
- Do people identify more with the overall organization or more with their particular unit or subgroup?

Behaviors are how the organization acts when deploying its plans. Consider:

- Do working units of people act more as independent individuals or more as interdependent teams?
- Is discipline more fluid and flexible or more structured?
- Do people have a bias more toward creating surprising break-throughs—big leaps—or more to making reliable, repeatable, steady progress?

Culture is an essential consideration in many of the tasks and tools you will deploy in your 100-Day Plan and beyond.

Netflix Reinvents Itself Again

Netflix received 34 Emmy Award nominations in 2015 for shows it created. Yet, a few short years before, it was purely a distribution channel, producing no content. This strategy shift represents a complete reinvention to take advantage of changing circumstances and opportunities.

It's the second time Netflix reinvented itself. A decade ago the growth of streaming videos threatened its video-by-mail delivery system. So it chose to keep the cannibals in the family, cut the heart out of its existing business model, and moved into streaming.

In some ways this is not surprising because its origins lay in cutting the heart out of Blockbuster's video store business model. The question is what allows an organization such as Netflix to reinvent itself and continue to grow while an organization such as Blockbuster can't get out of its own way.

The difference is culture. Blockbuster was more set in its ways, focused on protecting what it had and working to build reliable, repeatable processes in a structured, disciplined way. Its decision making was tightly controlled, and communication was so formal and directed as to leave little room for discussion.

On the other hand Netflix people talk about their culture like this: "Instead of a culture of process adherence, we have a culture of creativity and self-discipline, freedom and responsibility." Certainly they try to avoid "irrevocable disasters," but "mostly though, rapid recovery is the right model."[2]

Army versus Navy

As Boris Groysberg, Andrew Hill, and Toby Johnson describe in "Which of These People Is Your Future CEO?"[3] the U.S. Navy and Air Force are strong on process and light on flexibility, whereas the Army and Marines are lighter on process and stronger on flexibility. They argue these differences stem from the equipment with which the different services deploy. A small mistake on a ship can have devastating impact, as can not reacting to a changing situation in ground warfare. So the Navy has built a culture based on command and control to minimize mistakes whereas the Army has built one designed to push decisions down and out to encourage initiative.

Not surprisingly, when you look at the way the Army approaches behaviors, relationships, attitudes, values, and the environment, you get a markedly different picture than you do with the Navy. As you can see by the spider chart in Figure 1.1, the Army is more fluid, flexible, informal, and collaborative than the Navy on almost every dimension.

---

[2] Reed Hastings (Netflix's chief executive officer), 2009, "Culture," SlideShare, August 1.

[3] November, 2010, "Which of These People Is Your Future CEO? The Different Ways Military Experience Prepares Managers for Leadership," *Harvard Business Review*.

FIGURE 1.1　BRAVE Preferences

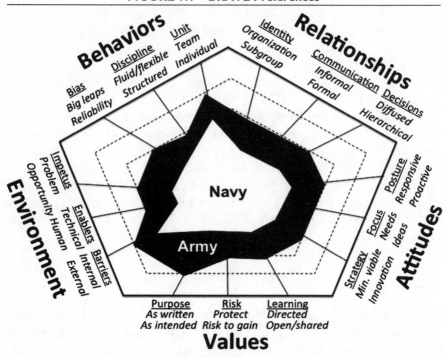

It's not that one is better than the other. It's just that they are different, appropriately so, given their different missions and circumstances.

This chart is based on Tool 1.1, which can help you map your culture. Like all the tools in this book, it is printed at the end of the chapter and included in the downloadable tools at www.onboardingtools.com. Most find it easier and more elegant to write in those than in the book. Plus, you'll find other tools and more in-depth discussions around a number of ideas on that site. The website is an important resource to accompany this book. Use it.

NOTE ON CULTURE

See Tool 1A.10 on www.onboardingtools.com for a discussion of culture across all the steps of onboarding. (Same material as in the book, just compiled into a single tool on BRAVE culture.)

Sell Before You Buy

Securing a new leadership position usually requires interviews. You can ace any interview if you remember three things during the process:

> Thing 1: You cannot turn down or accept a job offer that you have not received.
>
> Thing 2: There are only three fundamental interview questions—ever.
>
> Thing 3: There are only three fundamental interview answers—ever.

Thing 1

Before you accept a job, you must first get an offer. Then, and only then, can you decide whether you should accept it. Do not do these steps out of order. Your initial focus should be on getting the job offer. If you start to imagine or assume you have the job before you have the offer, you have diverted some of your energy away from reality and are wasting your time. Once you have received the offer, your approach should change.

Everything you do in the interview process should be designed to get someone else to offer you the job. This includes not only your answers to their questions but also your questions to them. At this stage in the process, your questions are not about helping you decide whether you want the job. They are about helping them decide to offer it to you. Sell yourself first. Secure the offer. Then, after you have the offer, and only then, figure out whether it's right for you.

Thing 2

There are only three interview questions.

Every question you've ever been asked, and every question you've ever asked in any interview, is a subset of one of these three fundamental questions:

1. Can you do the job?
2. Will you love the job?
3. Can I tolerate working with you?

Those three questions asked in a more traditional way are:

1. What are your strengths?
2. Will you be motivated to do the job?
3. Are you a fit?

That's it: strengths, motivation, fit. The questions may be asked in different ways, but every question, however worded, is just a variation on one of these. As each question comes, it is your task to determine which of the three is really being asked.

Thing 3

Because there are only three fundamental interview questions, there are only three fundamental interview answers.

Every answer you give in an interview should be a subset of these three answers:

1. My strengths are a match for this job.
2. My motivations are a match for this job.
3. I am a good fit for this organization.

That's it. Those three. Your answers to questions will be more elaborate, but your answers should always be dressed-up versions of one of the three.

Because there are only three interview questions and only three interview answers, all you have to do is to prepare three answers in advance and recognize what question you are being asked. Then you are ready to ace any interview.

The bad news is that it is going to be a lot more work than you might think to prepare these answers in advance of each interview. Interviews are exercises in solution selling. They are not about you. They are about your interviewers—their needs, their problems. You are the solution. Think of the interview process as a chance for you to show your ability to see, hear, and solve the organization's and the interviewer's problem.

If interviewers know what they are doing, they will be looking beyond a narrowly defined problem (and solution) and for technical expertise across a broader set of criteria: strengths, motivations, and fit. When they don't really know what they're doing, they can be brought around to seeing things the right way. Still, in every case the solution must be presented from their perspective. Thoughtful preparation can be the deciding factor between a yes and a no. This is tricky stuff, but it is worth the investment of time.

Question 1: Can you do the job? Or more likely: What are your strengths? (Strengths)

Answer 1: Prepare three situation/action/results examples that highlight your strengths in the areas most important over the short term and long term to the people interviewing you.

Question 2: Will you love the job? Or more likely: What are you looking to do? (Motivation)

Answer 2: Discuss how the role you are applying for matches what you like to do.

Question 3: Can I tolerate working with you? Or more likely: What sort of people do you like to work with? (Fit)

Answer 3: Discuss how your preferences across behaviors, relationships, attitudes, values, and the environment match the organization's culture on those dimensions.

Note you'll find more discussion about the questions behind the questions on www.onboardingtools.com.

Imagine that you are interviewing for a job where a new leader and a new team are being put together to solve a specific problem or to address a specific need or goal. To become the winning candidate, you may need to act as a management consultant, helping the decision makers and team members get a better sense of what the problems, or needs, really are, and then conveying confidence that under your supervision the right things will get done.

HOT TIP

Everything is part of the interview: You won't go too far wrong if you imagine that everything you do and say is being videotaped to be shown to the final decision maker. This is why you must use every part of every interaction with everybody in the organization as an opportunity to reinforce your strengths, motivation, and fit. Until you've been offered a job, it's all about getting the offer.

The Seven Deadly Land Mines

The first 100 days in your new role will be rife with land mines; just like the real thing, they are usually hidden and are often undetected until it is too late. Being aware that land mines exist and learning how to anticipate them will limit their devastating potential. Learning how to deactivate them safely will help you sail straight through to success (see Table 1.2).

Land mines will always exist but they are most easily hidden from you leading up to and through your first 100 days. Know that you must always be mitigating all of these land mines well beyond your transition.

WARNING!

What follows discusses these land mines one by one, but they frequently come in multiples and often interact with each other. Exposure to one risk heightens others, and failure has a way of gaining its own terrible and often unstoppable momentum.

Land Mine 1: Organization

The lack of a clear, concise, differentiating, and winning strategy creates an organizational land mine.

You do not want to get on a ship that is doomed to sink. Some people thrive on this risk and want to be part of the turnaround. It is one thing to be a turnaround expert going into an organization that knows it needs to make significant changes fast. It is a recipe for disaster if you are not a turnaround expert and you're going into an organization that needs those skills but doesn't actually realize it.

Louisa had been looking for a job for 18 months. She took a job with a growing division of a major player in the software business. It was trying to expand into a completely new area and asked her to come in as vice president of marketing for the new group. She had been lobbying for the general manager role, but settled for the marketing job because she was so excited about the new division's prospects. She should not have been.

As it turned out, the division had no competitive advantage and was competing against an entrenched competitor that had quickly

Table 1.2
Deadly Seven Onboarding Land Mines

Land Mines	Description	Best Stage to Mitigate/ Deactivate	Deactivation Method
Phase 1			
1. Organization	Lack of a winning strategy or the inability to implement that strategy	Before accepting job	Ask tough questions.
2. Role	Expectations and resources or key stakeholders are not aligned	Before accepting job	Listen for inconsistencies.
3. Personal skills	Gaps exist in your strengths, motivation, or fit.	Before accepting job	Ask yourself tough questions.
Phase 2			
4. Relationship	Failure to build or maintain key relationships, up, across, or down.	Between acceptance and start	Activate a 360-relationship compass and use it to help guide you through potential challenges.
5. Learning	Failure to gain adequate information, awareness, or knowledge of customers, collaborators, capabilities, competitors, or conditions.	Between acceptance and start	Activate an ongoing learning campaign to thoroughly master the 5Cs. Keep your learning sharp.
Phase 3			
6. Delivery	Failure to build a high-performing team or deliver results fast enough.	First 100 days	Identify and validate clear and genuine winning deliverables and timetable. Empower and execute with team.
7. Adjustment	Failure to see or react to situational changes	As appropriate	Monitor business conditions and results actively. Understand the causes of change. Replan and execute quickly.

stepped into the gap on which Louisa's new company had staked the division's future. Six months into the job, Louisa recommended that the company abandon the effort and focus its efforts on other things. It was the right recommendation for the organization, but bad for Louisa because she was out of a job again.

Deactivation method: Ask tough questions.

Land Mine 2: Role

If expectations, resources, or key stakeholders are not aligned, you will encounter a role land mine. Often new leaders step into jobs that are virtually impossible from the start because the expectations are unrealistic or cannot be delivered for whatever reason.

One new president had done a great job of negotiating his title and package, but had failed to consider reporting lines and resources. He soon learned that none of the heads of marketing, finance, information, or human resources reported to him. His only direct reports were the heads of sales and business development. By taking the title of president—without the appropriate authority—all he had managed to do was to paint a target on his back for his peers to shoot at so they could get him out of the way and strengthen their own positions.

Deactivation method: Listen for inconsistencies or uncertainty around your (1) role and responsibilities, (2) deliverables, (3) timetable, (4) authority, (5) interactions, and (6) access to essential resources.

Land Mine 3: Personal

Personal land mines are the ones that you bring to the new job. They are activated when significant gaps exist in your strengths, motivation, or fit for the job. Often executives assume that their strengths are well matched to a particular role, when in fact they are not. Assumptions about strengths usually are based on prior success without a true in-depth assessment of the match between strengths and the particular situation. Although a new job may sound like your former job, there will be a whole new range of dynamics that may require significantly different skill sets. By missing this factor, leaders often fail to realize that they may not possess certain strengths that are essential for success in the new role. But this is not you.

After years of working at large consumer product companies, Alice moved to Silicon Beach in Santa Monica, California, to join a start-up social networking site as the chief marketing officer. She was thrilled to be moving into a "hot new company," and she was thrilled with her promotion in title. Alice was hired to bring her experience in traditional marketing to the start-up. On her first day in the job, she called the marketing team together to ask for the market research studies, the most recent membership feedback, focus group results, the brand positioning strategy, and the current marketing strategy and category spend. She was shocked that none of that existed in the typical format and depth that she had grown accustomed to, if at all.

Alice knew that she had to make quick decisions on some key marketing areas, but she had no idea how to do that without her traditional tools or how to motivate a staff that was far different from the traditional marketing staff that she had worked with in the past. She struggled with the entrepreneurial environment and discovered that just being an expert in brand management was not enough to survive in a fast-paced, broken-field-run start-up. She struggled in almost everything she did and soon realized that the hot new company was not a fit for her motivations, her strengths, or her basic temperament. "I had the marketing skills, but I did not have any clue about the skills required in a start-up environment," she said.

Deactivation method: Ask yourself the tough questions about whether you really have the strengths, motivation, and fit required for success.

Land Mine 4: Relationship

If you fail to identify, establish, or maintain key relationships up, across, or down, you will encounter relationship land mines (There may be clusters of these, and they can set each other off in succession; watch out!). These key relationships are those that have a stake in or can impact your success. These stakeholders can be found up, down, or across the organization from you.

When you miss the needs or agendas of other key stakeholders or outside influencers, there is a good chance that some impact will be felt. The problem is you won't necessarily know that this has started to happen, but it can get a life and a momentum of its own outside of your presence or even awareness. If you lend an insufficient or ineffective effort to building a productive teamwork environment with direct reports, land mines are often the result. If expectations of up stakeholders are not clearly understood, go unchecked, or frequently change, this is certainly danger-ous territory for land mines. Finally, poor preparation and communica-tion follow-through are often key culprits in activating these land mines.

Relationship land mines catch many executives completely unaware. These are especially tricky because sometimes the results of stepping on one do not show up for months, or longer. What is worse, you can get caught by these land mines just by pure neglect of a key stakeholder or someone who you didn't even know should be a key stakeholder: "I was just too busy to reach out to her." "He has a role in all this? He's just the head of investor relations!"

Relationship risks are particularly severe for people who are brought in as change agents. Often those people come in with a hero mentality, thinking they are the organization's savior. This is not necessarily a problem and sometimes they're right. The problem occurs when new leaders *act* as if they are saviors. Nobody wants to see that, especially those who have been part of the situation that needs saving. Don't be a savior. Be a team leader. History is littered with many dead heroes who never made it home.

Sebastian came into the organization to create a new ventures group. He mapped out most of the key stakeholders and was building relationships with them. After a while, it became apparent that Suri, the head of another division, was undermining his efforts. Sebastian did not understand why, because he had never come in contact with Suri.

Eventually, Sebastian learned that Suri was upset that he had not seen her as important enough to establish a relationship with early on. She watched as he built relationships all around her and left her out. She felt he was purposely snubbing her. Suri was upset, not because of something Sebastian had done or said, but because he had not said anything to her at all. Her efforts to undermine him were an immature way of showing her disappointment, but she wanted him to know that she could make things difficult for him. Sebastian overlooked her when he built his key stakeholder list and it cost him months later.

Deactivation method: Activate a 360-relationship compass and use it to help guide you to potential challenges and land mines.

Land Mine 5: Learning

Fail to grasp key information in any of the 5Cs—customers, collabora-tors, capabilities, competitors, or conditions—and you have effectively created learning land mines. Executives often miss the importance of certain Cs or diminish the importance of one or more. If you don't have a learning plan in place for each and every C, the likelihood of undetected land mines greatly increases.

If you don't know what you need to know or—worse yet—don't know what you don't know, then land mines will surely be plentiful. So what do you need to know? At the very least, you need to know critical information about each of the 5Cs, especially about the real value chain of your business. If you use our guidelines for your 5Cs analysis, the information you gather will significantly diminish the risk of learning land mines.

Learning is essential. Being perceived as wanting to learn is almost as important as learning itself. You have heard it before: "Seek first to understand,"[4] "Don't come in with the answer,"[5] and "Wisdom begins in wonder."[6] You hear it repeatedly in many different ways, because it is proven advice. Heed it. You need to learn and you'll want to be perceived as being hungry to learn.

Harold joined a company that was helping companies take advantage of favorable tax treatments for new technologies. He had done his homework well across most of the 5Cs. He liked the team. They liked him. He knew exactly how he could add value to the group and to its customers. What he had failed to learn about was that the government was about to change the law and take away the favorable tax treatments. So, a few months into the job, the company effectively got legislated out of business.

Deactivation method: Activate an ongoing learning campaign to thoroughly master the 5Cs.

Land Mine 6: Delivery

In the end, it boils down to delivery. It's not what you do; it's the results you deliver. If you deliver, the organization can tolerate many other faults. If you are leading a team, you cannot deliver if the team does not deliver. At the end of your first 100 days, the most dangerous land mine

---

[4] Stephen Covey, 1989, *The 7 Habits of Highly Effective People*, (New York: Simon & Schuster).
[5] Michael Watkins, 2003, *The First 90 Days* (Boston: Harvard Business School Press).
[6] Attributed to Socrates.

is failing to build a high-performing team fast enough to deliver the expected results in the expected time frame.

Steve was hired as the head of business development for a venture-backed technology company that had developed a cutting-edge digital rights management (DRM) software. Steve was excited about the opportunity because he knew that the technology was one of the best and the market was screaming for such a DRM product that was easy and reliable to use. Steve's main priority was to enter into long-term agreements with the major entertainment studios.

Steve made inroads with the studios quickly, but he became frustrated by their notoriously slow movement. While keeping his eye on the studio business, he began to concentrate on other industries that required DRM technology and was able to secure a strong deal flow.

A year later Steve was fired after a meeting with the venture capital company. Although Steve was pleased with his inroads at the studios, he had not yet closed any deals with a major entertainment firm. He felt that the deal flow from other industries compensated, but he didn't understand that his up stakeholders thought he was concentrating 100 percent on studio business, which had far greater potential than the other industries that Steve had mined. He delivered, but he delivered off strategy.

Deactivation method: Identify clear and genuine winning deliverables and timetable. Validate with key stakeholders. Empower and execute with the team.

Land Mine 7: Adjustment

You can do everything correctly to this point, but if you do not see or react to the inevitable situational changes, then new land mines will certainly be created. The act of planning and managing is not a static exercise. You must be keenly aware of the fluid dynamics of your team's situation. Missing the need to survey the environment constantly and adjust accordingly is just like a skipper setting sail for a destination and never adjusting his or her sails for the ever-changing seas and weather conditions.

Things change and you and your team need to change when they do. Sometimes you can get away with minor adjustments. Sometimes a complete restart is required. The risk lies in not seeing the need to change, not understanding how to change effectively, or in being too slow to react to the changes you do see.

Tony was hired by Victor to run the operations of the division that Victor headed. Tony reported directly to Victor and soon after joining, he realized that the division was significantly underperforming. Tony embraced the challenge and made great gains in operational efficiencies in a short time; but while operations were improving, other aspects of the division continued to falter. As a result, Wendy, one of Victor's counterparts from a sister division, was promoted to head both divisions. So now, Tony was reporting to Victor, who was reporting to Wendy. Tony thought that this move represented no big change for him.

He was wrong. He was sure that Victor would represent his work to Wendy, and he assumed that his style and approach would be embraced because it was producing results. What he did not know was that Wendy's division had been run under a completely different operational style and her division's results were far stronger than Victor's ever had been.

For Tony, the new reporting structure was a sea change, indicating that a huge adjustment was required. Tony underestimated the magnitude of the change, and therefore it never crossed his mind that a "huge adjustment" might be required. Any change in structure requires a relook at what is going on, if not a complete restart. Tony did not do that. He kept soldiering on, assuming that Victor would make his case to Wendy.

Two months later Victor and everyone he had brought in to work for him, including Tony, were fired.

Deactivation method: Monitor business conditions, results, and organization changes actively. Understand the causes and implications of change. Replan and execute quickly.

You've got a choice. You can leverage our suggested approach to uncover and help you assess and mitigate those risks. Or, you can send us an e-mail later saying, "I wish I'd read this chapter before I accepted that job!" You won't be alone.

Do Your Due Diligence Before You Accept the Job Offer

Should I take this job? To know the answer to that question, you need to make an informed assessment of the degree of risk. Almost nobody wants to do due diligence. Almost nobody likes to do due diligence. Almost nobody knows how to do due diligence well. It's as though people don't want to do anything to spoil the moment of getting a job offer. Ignorance can be bliss. Until the things you didn't see show up and conk you on the head.

At the core, due diligence is an exercise in collecting and analyzing information from multiple sources to understand the risk inherent in a decision. As with just about everything discussed in this book, a carefully thought out and methodical approach will help.

Mitigate Risk Before You Accept a Job

To avoid trying to boil the ocean, you've got to focus your risk assessment on exploring the few most important areas. Before accepting a job, you must gather information in the following areas to answer three fundamental questions around organization, role, and personal risks.

Organizational Risk

When looking to identify organizational risk, be sure to assess risk elements across the 5Cs: customers, collaborators, capabilities, competitors, and conditions. The good news is that you probably have a significant head start on understanding many of these, or you wouldn't even have been considered for the job. But do not rely on what you think you know.

The goal is to build an understanding of customers, collaborators, capabilities, competitors, and conditions to help you understand the organization's strengths and weaknesses. Tool 1.3 provides more detailed guidance for your 5Cs analysis. Go through the exercise and use these thought starters to see what new things you can learn. Here are some headlines about the 5Cs to help trigger insightful questions for you to ask.

Customers: First line, customer chain, end users, influencers

Collaborators: Suppliers, allies, government/community leaders

Capabilities: Human, operational, financial, technical, key assets

Competitors: Direct, indirect, potential

Conditions: Social/demographic, political/government/regulatory, economic, market

The main questions you should answer with the 5Cs analysis are:

What is the organization's sustainable competitive advantage?

Are there any risks with the current *Customer* base?

Are there any risks with relationships with significant *Collaborators* of the organization?

Does the organization have the *Capabilities* required for long-term success?

Do *Competitors* pose significant risks to the viability of the organization?

Are there any outside *Conditions* that will impact the viability of the organization?

See Tool 1.4 on situational assessment for a strengths, weaknesses, opportunities, and threats (SWOT) analysis.

Role Risk

The main questions you should answer here are:

Did anyone have concerns about this role, and if so, what was done to mitigate them?

Why does the position exist? Why did the organization need to create it in the first place?

What are the objectives and outcomes? What are you supposed to get done? By when is it supposed to be done?

What will the impact be on the rest of the organization? What kind of interactions can you expect with key stakeholders?

What are your specific responsibilities, including decision-making authority and direct reports?

To mitigate the first risk (internal concerns about the role), you should:

1. Find the people who had concerns.
2. Understand those concerns.
3. Understand what has changed to make those concerns go away.

4. Believe those people will support the role (and you) going forward, but keep a close eye on their actions to verify.

To mitigate the remaining risks and understand key elements about the role itself, you should ensure that the key stakeholders:

1. Are aligned around the role's reason to exist.
2. Understand and are in agreement with the objectives of the role.
3. Understand the impact that the role will have on them and the organization.
4. Are clear on the responsibilities of the role.
5. Understand the interdependencies that the role requires and that their relevant constituents will have the elements of the new role communicated to them in an appropriately thorough way.

Personal Risk

The main questions you should answer here are:

> What, specifically, about me, led the organization to offer me the job?
>
> Is this the company and role that can best capitalize on my strengths over time?
>
> Will I look forward to coming to work three weeks, months, or years from now?
>
> Where do my preferences fall along the BRAVE scale?
> - Use Tool 1.1 to record your own personal BRAVE preferences.
>   Will I fit with the culture?
> - Use Tool 1.1 to assess how you think the new organization rates (based on what you know now) along the BRAVE preferences.
> - Compare and contrast your preferences to those of the organization to determine fit.

The objective is to understand how closely your strengths, motivation, and fit match what is required to deliver the expected results. Knowing what you know, would you hire yourself for the job? If your assessment indicates that there might not be a fit, you should seriously consider walking away. Executives often convince themselves that they can make themselves fit but that approach rarely works.

In your efforts to understand these risks, you'll want multiple potential sources of information. You'll need scouts and spies to help you. Scouts are people outside the company who can give you a view of what's going on inside the company. Spies are people on the inside who can give you special insight into the organization and its environment. Look to these allies for supplemental information across the 5Cs to round out your understanding of the situation.

Now What?

You've gathered your information. You've analyzed it and thought about it. Now what do you do? Categorize the risk as low, manageable, mission crippling, or insurmountable and then take appropriate action.

- If the overall risk is **low**, move forward—keeping your eyes open for things you've missed or things that change.
- If the risk is **manageable**, move forward, managing the risks as you go.
- You cannot succeed in the face of a **mission crippling** risk until you've figured out how to mitigate the risk. The critical judgment in this exercise is separating manageable risk from mission crippling risk.
- If the risk is **insurmountable**, a mission crippling risk that cannot be mitigated, walk away.

Note you'll find some additional thoughts on risk mitigation and negotiating as well as an onboarding risk calculator at www .onboardingtools.com.

Position Yourself for Success: Summary and Implications

- **Culture**—Understand your own cultural preferences and strengths in the context of potential job opportunities.

- **Sell before you buy**—Get the offer first. You cannot turn down an offer you have not received. So sell before you buy, positioning your strengths, motivation, and fit in the context of the interviewing organization's needs.

- **Due diligence**—Do a real due diligence before accepting, understanding the level of risk you face across the seven deadly land mines (organization, role, personal, relationship, learning, delivery, and adjustment).

- **Manage risk**—Manage that risk appropriately with the help you need.

QUESTIONS YOU SHOULD ASK YOURSELF

Do I have examples to support my answers to the three interview questions?

Have I done sufficient due diligence?

Am I clear on my strengths with regard to this role?

Am I clear on my cultural preferences? How do my preferences compare with the organization's culture?

Is the job right for me in terms of strength, motivation, and fit?

Do I understand the risks and have I thought through my approach to manage those risks?

Additional Articles and Tools on www.onboardingtools.com

TOOL 1.1
BRAVE Culture
Assessment/Preference[*]

For each of the components below, estimate on a scale of 1–5, where 1 means the text in the middle column completely describes the preference and 5 means the text in the right column completely describes the preference, where your and the organization's culture preferences fall. Add and score other subcomponents as you identify them. Identify the most important gaps and determine whether or how the gaps can be bridged.

Environment—Where to Play

1. Impetus:	Opportunity to capture	Problem to solve
2. Enablers:	Human/interpersonal/ societal	Technical/mechanical/ scientific
3. Barriers:	External hurdles	Internal capabilities
Other insights:		

Values—What Matters and Why

1. Interpretation of mission, vision, values:	As intended (evolving)	As written (set)
2. Risk appetite:	Risk more/gain	Protect what is
3. Learning:	Open/shared	Directed
Underlying beliefs:		

Attitude—How to Win

1. Strategy:	Premium price/service/ innovation	Low cost/self-service/ min. viable
2. Focus:	Ideas out	Customer needs in
3. Posture:	Proactive	Responsive
Other observations:		

(continued)

TOOL 1.1   BRAVE Culture Assessment/Preference (continued)

Relationships—How to Connect

1. Power, decision making:	Diffused/debated	Controlled/monarchical
2. Communication, controls:	Informal/verbal/ face-to-face	Formal/directed/written
Identity:	Overall organization	Unit/subgroup
Others:		

Behaviors—What Impact

1. Working units:	Independent individuals	Interdependent teams
2. Discipline:	Fluid/flexible	Structured/disciplined
3. Bias:	Surprising breakthroughs	Reliable/repeatable/ steady progress
Others:		

TOOL 1.2
Risk Assessment[*]

For each of the components below, estimate the level of risk for each land mine on a scale of 1 to 4. Then look at the individual rankings to come up with an overall risk assessment.

Risk level scale:

1: Low

2: Manageable

3: Mission crippling

4: Insurmountable

Organization: Assess risks of organization's strategy and ability to implement (1-2-3-4):

(Look for the organization's sustainable competitive advantage.)

Role: Assess risks of stakeholders' alignment around expectations and resources (1-2-3-4):

(Understand who had concerns about the role and what was done to address them.)

Personal: Assess risk of gaps in your strengths, motivation, or fit (1-2-3-4):

(Understand what, specifically, about you led to your getting an offer.)

Relationships: Assess risks in your ability to build and maintain key relationships (1-2-3-4):

Learning: Assess risks in your ability to gain adequate information and knowledge (1-2-3-4):

Delivery: Assess risks in your ability to build a high-performing team that can deliver fast enough (1-2-3-4):

Adjustment: Assess risks in your ability to see or react to situational changes down the road (1-2-3-4):

(continued)

TOOL 1.2   Risk Assessment (continued)

Overall Risk: Assess overall risk by looking all the land mines combined (1-2-3-4):

If the overall risk assessment is rated:

1. Low, then do nothing out of the ordinary (but keep your eyes open for the inevitable changes).
2. Manageable, then manage it in the normal course of your job.
3. Mission crippling, then resolve it before accepting the job or mitigate it before doing anything else.
4. Insurmountable, then walk away.

TOOL 1.3
5Cs Situation Analysis*

Use this tool for guidance in your due diligence to build an understanding of customers, collaborators, capabilities, competitors, and conditions to help you understand the organization's strengths and weaknesses.

1. **Customers** (First line, customer chain, end users, influencers)
   Needs, hopes, preferences, commitments, strategies, price/value perspective by segment:

First-Line/Direct Customers
- Universe of opportunity—total market, volume by segment
- Current situation—volume by customer; profit by customer

Customer Chain
- Customers' customers—total market, volume by segment
- Current customers' strategies, volume and profitability by segment

End Users
- Preference, consumption, usage, loyalty, and price value data and perceptions for our products and competitors' products

Influencers
- Key influencers of customer and end user purchase and usage decisions

2. **Collaborators** (Suppliers, business allies, partners, government/community leaders)
   - Strategies, profit/value models for external and internal stakeholders (up, across, and down)

(continued)

TOOL 1.3   5Cs Situation Analysis (continued)

3. Capabilities

- Human (Style and quality of management, strategy dissemination, culture: values, norms, focus, discipline, innovation, teamwork, execution, urgency, politics)
- Operational (Integrity of business processes, effectiveness of organizational structure, links between measures and rewards, corporate governance)
- Financial (Capital and asset utilization and investor management)
- Technical (Core processes, information technology systems, supporting skills)
- Key assets (Brands and intellectual property)

4. Competitors (Direct, indirect, potential)

- Strategies, profit/value models, profit pools by segment, source of pride

5. Conditions

- Social/demographic—trends
- Political/government/regulatory—trends
- Economic—macro and micro—trends
- Market definition, inflows, outflows, substitutes—trends

Pulling It Together: SWOT Analysis and Thinking about

- Sources, drivers, hinderers of revenue, and value.
- Current strategy/resource deployment: Coherent? Adequate? De facto strategy?
- Insights and scenarios (To set up: What/So what/Now what?)

TOOL 1.4
SWOT*

Use this tool to complete a robust SWOT analysis, as shown in Figure 1.2.

FIGURE I.2   SWOT

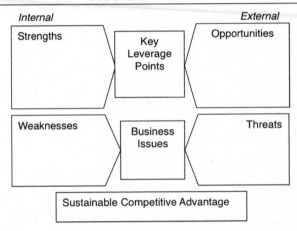

Strengths: Internal to organization—things we do better

Weaknesses: Internal to organization—things we do worse

Opportunities: External to organization—things to capitalize on

Threats: External to organization—things to worry about

Key Leverage Points
Opportunities we can leverage our strengths against (where to play to win)

Business Implications
Threats our weaknesses make us vulnerable to (where to play not to lose)

Sustainable Competitive Advantages
Key leverage points that can be sustained over extended periods

---

CHAPTER 2

Leverage the Fuzzy Front End

JUMP-START RELATIONSHIPS. LISTEN, LEARN, AND PLAN BEFORE DAY ONE.

WARNING!

If you have already started your new role, this chapter may upset you. It is full of ideas for people to implement before they start. The best way to take charge, build your team, and get great results faster than anyone thought possible is to create time by starting earlier than anyone thought you would.

But even if you have already started your new role, read this chapter. If you have yet to tackle the things presented in this chapter, start doing them immediately. Read on to find out where you need to catch up.

Create Time, Take Action

Many leaders fall into the trap of thinking that leadership begins on Day One of a new job. Like it or not, a new leader's role begins as soon as that person is an acknowledged candidate for the job. Everything new leaders do and say and don't do and don't say will send powerful signals, starting well before they even walk in the door on Day One.

If you embrace this concept and do something about it, you increase your chances of success. This one idea can make or break a new leader's transition. New leaders who miss the opportunity to get a head start before the start often discover later that organizational or market momentum was working against them even before they showed up for their first full day at the office.

This bonus time between acceptance and start is the Fuzzy Front End. It often comes at the worst possible time, interfering with the last days of an old job, time earmarked for taking a vacation, catching up with personal errands postponed for too long, or just unwinding a little before the big day.

The good news is that, more often than not, the key elements of the Fuzzy Front End can be addressed in relatively short order. Even so, strive to stretch out the time between acceptance and your start date and get as much done as you can. This is the only opportunity you'll ever have to create extra time and valuable white space[1] before jumping into your new role.

Choose the Right Day to Be Day One

One subtle way of creating time is to take control of the start date. If there's flexibility—which is not always the case—you might negotiate a start date that allows a longer Fuzzy Front End and therefore more time for helpful activities before Day One. Alternatively, you might separate your actual first day on the payroll from the officially announced first day. By having a private Day One that your boss knows about and a later public Day One, you can accomplish things while you are an employee but before you start getting pulled into the normal day-to-day routine, thereby stretching your Fuzzy Front End.

---

[1] See Malcolm Gladwell, 2005, *Blink* (Boston: Little, Brown).

The Longer the Better

At first, Nathaniel did not buy the concept that he should start before his official Day One. He wanted to take some time off so that he could show up at his new job rested and relaxed. Further, he felt uncomfortable asking for meetings before he was officially on the job. Eventually he agreed to try several of our suggested actions before Day One.

Here is exactly what he wrote to us in an e-mail one week later:

> I've already reached out to some future colleagues and some agency counterparts just to introduce myself. You're right—it is game changing. Everyone has reacted with warmth and candor, and it will make the first few weeks far more effective and enjoyable.

As laid out in Tool 2.1, the 100-Day Plan Worksheet, make your Fuzzy Front End even more powerful with these six steps:

1. Determine your leadership approach given the context and culture you face.
2. Identify key stakeholders.
3. Craft your entry message using current best thinking.
4. Jump-start key relationships and accelerate your learning.
5. Manage your personal and office setup.
6. Plan your Day One, early days, and first 100 days.

1. Determine Your Leadership Approach Given the Context and Culture You Face

Step one is to identify the need for change and the readiness for change. The context you're facing determines how fast you *should* move. (Need for change.) The current culture determines how fast and effectively you *can* move. (Readiness for change.) The key question is: How significantly and how fast does the organization need to change given its business environment, history, and recent performance?

Business Environment: You already assessed the business environment with your 5Cs analyses during due diligence. Be sure to look for trends within each C: customers, collaborators, capabilities, competitors, and conditions.

Organization History: Understanding how the organization got to its current state can give you invaluable insight into the drivers for change as well as the roots of individual team members' assumptions about the situation. Go back as far as you can to understand things such as the founder's intent, heroes along the way, and the stories and myths that people carry around with them. Has the culture continually evolved? Are employees protective of the culture?

Recent Business Performance: Dig below the obvious in looking at recent business performance. Understand the components of the overall numbers to get at what is working well and less well. We've seen a number of cases where favorable overall revenue growth was either misleading (reflecting one-off wins versus true share growth) or masked underlying problems in one or more core business units or irreversible rises in cost. Identify absolute and relative results, recent trends, positive and negative drivers, and whether they are temporary blips or enduring obstacles. Use Tool 2.2 to help with your context assessment.

Compare Role Expectations to Context Analysis

Now compare the expectations/objectives that have been explained to you (for your role and team) by those you met during interviews and due diligence against your analysis of the business environment, the organization's history, and the recent business performance to determine how well (or, poorly) positioned the organization is to achieve those objectives. Are those expectations out of whack with the current business environment, the way the company has historically operated, or recent business performance? This will give you a sense of how fast things need to change.

In a postacquisition or merger integration, the task of assessing the need for change is determined by the strengths, momentum, and objectives of the combined businesses, as well as which specific changes need to be made during integration to achieve these objectives. The rationale for merging entities varies. Some are driven by cost benefits, calling for rapid functional integration and job eliminations. Others are driven by revenue growth potential from diversification, calling for minimal or zero integration, or by incremental investments to accelerate growth. Different situations will have different contexts and therefore call for very different approaches to integration and change.

Look at the Culture to Determine the Readiness for Change

Now that you have determined the organization's need for change, it is time to assess the organization's cultural readiness to accept, embrace, and adapt to change. Readiness to change requires a combination of self-awareness, will, and skill. Members of the organization must understand the need for change, have the desire to change, and have the ability to change.

Your first look at this will be derived from the cultural assessment you did during your due diligence (or should do now). When working with merging or newly reorganized teams, remember to assess the readiness for change for the combined or new organization, starting with the new leadership team.

HOT TIP

Look well beyond the professed culture: It's not that people lie about their preferences. It's just that value statements and creeds are often aspirational. You must understand the norms of behaviors, relationships, attitudes, values, and the work environment that people default to "when the boss is not around."

Determine Your Leadership Approach

At this point you, you've assessed whether cultural change is needed and whether the team is ready. Now you are ready to choose how to best engage with the existing culture by assimilating, converging and evolving, or shocking the organization (ACES).

After the decision to take the job in the first place, this may be the most important decision you make in your first 100 days. It is difficult, if not impossible, to recover from a wrong cultural engagement choice. Your choice is dependent upon the environment you're walking into and the existing culture's readiness for change. Tool 2.3 will help you determine the most appropriate approach for your situation as illustrated in Figure 2.1.

Assimilate when your analysis indicates that *urgent change is not required* to deliver the expected results and yet the readiness for change exists as reflected in a cohesive team in place. You can figure out the

FIGURE 2.1   Context and Culture

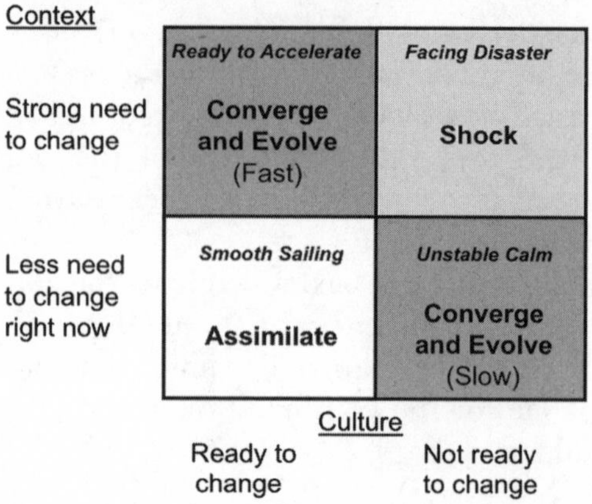

Context

	Ready to Accelerate	Facing Disaster
Strong need to change	**Converge and Evolve** (Fast)	**Shock**
Less need to change right now	*Smooth Sailing* **Assimilate**	*Unstable Calm* **Converge and Evolve** (Slow)

Culture

Ready to change	Not ready to change

minor changes you need to make over time together with your team and your stakeholders. This is a wonderful but rare situation.

In most cases you'll want to converge and evolve.

Converge and Evolve *slowly* when your analysis indicates that *urgent change is not required* but slight adjustments will be needed over time to deliver the expected results yet the *culture is not ready to change* to support the required adjustments. First become part of the organization, and then slowly start to implement the changes that are required. Often a way to start this change is with a series of carefully thought through step changes, deployed over time.

Converge and Evolve *quickly* when your analysis indicates that significant changes are required immediately to deliver expected results and the *culture is ready* for change. You may be the catalyst that helps the organization wake up to the urgent need for change. *Quickly* is the word—too slow and failure will catch you.

Shock when *significant changes must be made immediately* to deliver the expected results and when the culture is *not ready* to change. In this scenario, you have a truly challenging situation. You must shock the system for it to survive. You must do it immediately. And the going will be tough. Know that this is extraordinarily risky and that you may end up as a dead hero, paving the way for your successor to complete a transformation you couldn't survive yourself.

When leading teams about to be merged or reorganized, *converge and evolve* is almost always the best approach. Pure *assimilation* will be too slow, and the benefits of synergies may never be realized. If you deploy a *shock* approach, you will miss the opportunity to clarify roles and enroll new players in the definition of future state. Remember—people will not pay attention to anything to do with strategy or execution until they know what *their own role* will be in the new organization.

It is critical to get this right. Think this through early, use your best preliminary assessment to decide your leadership approach, test your hypothesis during your Fuzzy Front End and then reassess your choice just before Day One.

2. Identify Key Stakeholders

Step two of the Fuzzy Front End is to identify your key stakeholders. These are the people who can have the most impact on your success in your new role. Many transitioning executives fail to think through this process or look in only one direction to find their key stakeholders. Others make the mistake of treating everyone the same and end up trying to please all of them.

Up stakeholders may include your boss, your indirect boss if there is a matrix organization, your boss's boss, the board of directors, your boss's assistant, or anyone else who resides further up in the organization.

Across stakeholders might include key allies, peers, partners, and even the person who wanted your job but didn't get it. The across stakeholders that executives often forget are key clients and customers (external and internal).

Down stakeholders usually include your direct reports and other critical support people who are essential to successful implementation of your team's goals. Your executive assistants should be high on this list, because they can often serve as additional sets of eyes and ears.

Former stakeholders: If you're getting promoted from within or making a lateral move, make sure to take into account your up, across, and down stakeholders from your former position.

Internal board: Your internal board is made up of the people you are going to treat differently because of their influence or impact regardless of their explicit roles in the hierarchy. You're going to treat them like board members, never surprising them in meetings and making sure that they get the chance to give you informal, off-the-record advice. Set the stage early and position yourself as an executive who is eager for and welcomes feedback from your internal board.

Some key stakeholders will be apparent, yet others are often hidden from view, so do not be afraid to ask your human resources contact, boss, predecessor, buddy, or mentor when you are building your list. Throughout, have a bias to keep more people on the list rather than less—at least to start. Ignoring a key stakeholder can have a devastating impact on a new leader and might kill any chance of a successful transition.

Similarly, have a bias to treat people with more respect rather than less. If you are unsure where stakeholders fit on your list, it's always better to upgrade a stakeholder. You are not going to get in much trouble treating an *across* like an *up* or a *down* like an *across*. The opposite is not true.

Inevitably some of these stakeholders will support what you're trying to do, some will resist it, and some will sit on the sidelines and watch for a while. Call them contributors, detractors, and watchers, respectively.

Contributors: These are the people who share your vision and have been working for change. Often they are new to the company or role, so they see that there's more to gain by going forward with the new leaders than by holding on to the past.

Detractors: These are the people who are comfortable with the status quo, fear looking incompetent, perceive a threat to their values/power, fear negative consequences for their key allies, and have been in the position for a long time, so they have more to lose in giving up the current state than they have to gain in supporting a risky change.

Watchers: These are the people who are on the fence, generally the silent majority.

Note that people with high levels of current power have a bias to resist change because they have more to lose than to gain as illustrated in Figure 2.2 below. It's not always the case, but it is true in enough situations for you to be particularly thoughtful in developing relationships with these people.

The overall prescription is to move every influencer one step in the right direction. Don't try to turn detractors into contributors in one fell swoop. In general, start by increasing the commitment level of your contributors. Then move the convincible watchers into contributors. And get the detractors out of the way.

In any case, you will want to answer the following questions about your audience:

- With whom are you communicating? Be as specific as you can, and include everyone and all groups that can have an impact, including your target, their primary influencers, and other influencers.

FIGURE 2.2   Power and Change

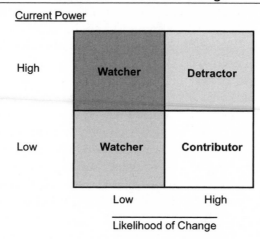

Current Power

High	Watcher	Detractor
Low	Watcher	Contributor
	Low	High

Likelihood of Change

Answer each one of the following questions with your entire target audience in mind:

- What are they currently thinking and doing? What's most important to them?
- What do they need to stop doing, keep doing, or change how they are doing?
- What do they need to know to move them from their current state to the desired state?

3. Craft Your Entry Message Using Your Current Best Thinking

Step three of the Fuzzy Front End is to craft your entry message. Before you start talking to any of your stakeholders, you'll want to clarify your initial message.

Everything you do communicates, especially in the Fuzzy Front End and the first interactions with people after you start. *Everything* you do and say and don't do and don't say sends powerful signals to everybody in the organization observing you and everyone in the organization who is in communication with those who observe you.

This works in both directions. Be keenly aware that everything you experience is, or should be, communicating something to you as well. Hard data, relationships, inferences, your intuition, existing communication material, and what you might see between the lines all provide clues as to how you should begin to craft your message. Not only are you communicating with your new environment and colleagues, but you are also absorbing what they are communicating.

Make no mistake about it; your communication starts in the Fuzzy Front End (if not before) whether you realize it or not. If you're not sure about your entry message at this point, stop and think it through. You don't have to stick with it. Most likely you won't because it will evolve to become more precise as you learn. But you must have a point of view going in if you're going to lead. Your message is the keystone of your communication. Your entry message is the starting point. It should be enough to satisfy your key stakeholders' curiosity while optimizing your opportunities for learning.

Crafting and deploying your message has to do with the words you use (and don't) and the actions you take (and don't). Be conscious of your choices and craft an intentional entry message before you start talking to stakeholders. You are going to get positioned in people's minds either by what others tell them about you or by what you say and do. You're always better off taking control of as much of that as you can. This requires an entry message about the change—which you will evolve as you learn.

Put a stake in the ground with your current best thinking to craft your entry message. Use that to help with your directed learning and evolve as you learn.

As you start your new role, recall that you can't get people to do anything different unless they believe that there is a reason for them to do it (platform for change), they can picture themselves in a better place (vision), and they know what their part is (call to action). Your communication points flow from your message, the platform for change, the vision, and the call to action.

1. **Platform for change (Why):** The things that will make your audience realize they need to do something different from what they have been doing. (Note people react better to an external platform for change outside their control than to being told that something they are doing is not good enough.)

2. **Vision (What):** Picture of a brighter future—that your audience can picture themselves in. Not your vision. Theirs.

3. **Call to action (How):** Actions the audience can take to get there so they can be part of the solution.

Once you have thought these foundational points through, distill them down to one driving message and your main communication points. Don't ever forget that your audience is always asking, "What does this mean for me?" Use the "Message" section in Tool 2.1 to capture this information.

When John stepped into the role to create a division to capitalize on new growth opportunities, his entry message was clear, concise, and compelling:

- Our competition has jumped ahead of us in technology solutions. If we stand still, we will continue to lose share, profits, and our ability to invest (Platform for Change).

- We have been given the cash to acquire leading technology businesses in our space, which will embed our content in our customers' systems and leapfrog us past the competition (Vision).

- Our goal is to identify the right businesses to acquire and to define a new way of integrating them so that we can preserve their strengths and differentiate us from the competition—permanently (Call to Action).

As a result of this compelling message, John was able to attract top talent from inside the company and convince attractive businesses to sell to his firm and join his team. The team achieved more than 20 percent growth and favorably changed the competitive playing field for the parent company.

HOT TIP

Get your message vaguely right immediately. Of course you're not going to go preach your message on or before Day One. You're going to evolve it over time. But you can't avoid inadvertently sending the wrong message until you know the right message for you, for them, for the mission, and for the moment.

4. Jump-Start Key Relationships and Accelerate Your Learning Before Day One

Step four of the Fuzzy Front End is to jump-start key relationships and accelerate your learning. These two items work hand in hand. You achieve this by conducting prestart meetings and phone calls *now*, before you start. The impact you can make by reaching out to critical stakeholders before you start is incalculable. Yet some executives are surprisingly reluctant to set up those meetings. They often expect to encounter resistance, but rarely do.

First, using your list of key stakeholders, determine which ones you should speak with before Day One. The most important stakeholders are the ones who are going to be most critical to your surviving and thriving in the new role.

These might include:

- Your new boss
- The most influential board members
- Critical peers—especially ones who were candidates for your new job
- Critical customers and clients
- Critical direct reports—especially ones who were candidates for your new job or who are considered flight risks

To make the process easier, here are some suggestions for starting a conversation:

> "Hi Jack, I'm Jill. I'll be starting in two weeks as president. Stuart has told me that you're an absolutely critical part of the team. I didn't want to show up without getting a chance to meet you in advance."

> "Bob, since you're such a valued customer of my new company, I can't imagine starting work without getting to know you first. I'll meet you anytime, anywhere in the world that's most convenient for you, over the next month. I'd really like to have your perspective on what's going on before I start."

> "Andrew, since you weren't on the board's search committee, we haven't met. But I'd like to spend some time with you before I start."

Leverage the Fuzzy Front End to Get Real Answers and Perspective

Another reason to start communicating with key stakeholders early is that the answers you get to questions before you actually start will be different from the answers you get after you start. You are a different person before you start. You are not yet an employee or boss. You are just someone looking to make a connection and learn. The answers you get during the Fuzzy Front End almost always prove exceedingly valuable after Day One.

What You See as Possible Just Might Define You

You should have meetings with the most important key stakeholders up, across, and down as well as phone calls with other stakeholders, if at all possible. This is so important that you should expand your concept of *possible*. Some executives have flown halfway around the world for hour-long meetings and met key stakeholders on ski lifts, cruise ships, Little League baseball fields, and the hinterlands just to get those meetings done before Day One. Get creative.

There are times when Fuzzy Front End meetings may not be possible or a potential stakeholder may be unwilling. Even so, just asking for the premeeting makes a favorable impact.

Prestart Conversations Have a Cascading Impact

Bill was joining a company as head of sales. Jairu, the previous, beloved head of sales had switched over to head up client relations with the firm's largest customer. Bill had what he thought was a nice but not particularly important conversation with Jairu on the Sunday before he started.

The next day, Bill's Day One, six of his eight direct reports said that Jairu had called them the evening before. They each told Bill that Jairu had told them that he thought Bill was a "good guy" who would be an asset. Jairu could have made the transition difficult. Instead, Bill had turned him into a supporter—even before Day One.

HOT TIP

Meet with critical stakeholders before you start. This one idea is worth a gazillion times whatever you paid for this book. Contacting key stakeholders before you start always makes a huge difference. It is a game changer.

Accelerate Your Learning

Now that you have your prestart conversations set, it is important to have an approach for those conversations. Make no mistake; these conversations are most successful when you are talking as little as possible and listening as attentively as possible. They are about building relationships and learning.

In a wonderful Technology, Education, Design (TED) Talk, researcher/storyteller Brené Brown explained that making a connection with someone else requires us to let him or her really see us, leaving ourselves vulnerable to harm.[2] These early prestart conversations are your first best chance to let your guard down, be vulnerable, and make connections with your most important stakeholders by asking for their help in terms of their read on the situation, priorities, and "how things are done around here."

Because this is about relationships first, your first question will probably be something along the lines of "Tell me about yourself." You want to connect with your key stakeholders individually. You want to understand their personal wants and needs as well as their business issues. This may also be a good time to take your crafted message out for a test drive; but keep in mind this is not about you, so keep your message short and on point. Because you are here to build relationships and learn, it is not the time to tell your life story or to offer opinions on how things should be done.

Structuring the conversations is useful. Come into these conversations with an open mind, and actively listen to what your key stakeholders have to say. Doing so in a planned and thoughtful way is fundamental to maximizing the value of these conversations. Break the conversations into learning, expectations, and implementation. Tool 2.5 will help.

Strengths and Perceptions

Start this part by probing people's read on the general situation. Focus on two key areas: strengths and perceptions. Ask people what strengths and capabilities are required for success versus their perceptions of what is in place now. Notice the differences. This is not a search for the one truth. This is an exercise in understanding the different stakeholders' perceptions so you can better lead and communicate with them once you take charge.

---

[2] 2010, "The Power of Vulnerability," TED Talk video, 20:19. June.

When you receive answers to your questions, ask for examples that might reinforce the answers. We all communicate with stories. Beginning in the Fuzzy Front End, drop any reference to your former organization, and switch to *we* conversations about your new organization immediately. If you manage these conversations well, you should have several *we* stories to choose from going forward.

Storytelling is one of the most powerful communication tools. As Peter Guber describes in his article on "The Four Truths of the Storyteller,"[3] the most impactful stories embody:

1. **Truth to the teller:** sharing and conveying the deepest values with openness and candor
2. **Truth to the audience:** tapping into what's important and delivering on what is emotionally fulfilling for them
3. **Truth to the mission:** driving toward a purpose that is meaningful and rewarding for the teller and for the audience
4. **Truth in the moment:** fitting into the appropriate context for each audience, each time

Take note that the core element is truth.

Keep in mind that the story itself is not enough. You must live the story. Your followers won't really believe what you show or say; they will believe only what you actually do. This is why storytelling is necessary but not sufficient by itself. This is why it's so important to live your message. You must model the attitudes and behaviors you want others to follow so those others can share your understanding and your dreams, feelings, and commitment. This starts with your initial contacts—even before you start.

Expectations

The objectives of the conversations with your stakeholders will be different up, across, and down. Therefore, your questions will also be different for each group. Your *up* stakeholders' expectations around priorities and resources are direction for you. Your *across* stakeholders' expectations are input to build mutual understanding. Your *down* stakeholders' expectations are data to help you learn about their current reality and their needs.

---

[3] 2008, *Harvard Business Review*, January.

This is also an excellent time to figure out if there are any *untouchables*. Untouchables are those things that may seem odd or do not have a natural fit with the larger goals of an organization or division, but might be pet projects or protected people that you should not touch. Most organizations have them; and they can be the third rail for executives who don't recognize them as untouchables. Identify them early and let them be—at least at first.

Implementation

At this part of the conversation, you're looking to understand (1) control points (what things are measured, tracked, and reported and how), (2) how decisions are made, and (3) the best way to communicate with people.

Different organizations use different metrics and processes for controlling what is really going on. You'll need to understand what things are measured, tracked, and reported and how—and what is not being formally tracked but informally watched in the shadows.

Understanding how decisions are made is about understanding who makes what decisions with whose input. There are five ways that you and another person can make decisions:

Level 1: I decide on my own.

Level 2: I decide with input from you.

Level 3: You and I decide together.

Level 4: You decide with my input.

Level 5: You decide on your own.

In general, you want to push decisions to Levels 2 and 4 (either you or your key stakeholder makes decisions with input from the other). Input is helpful whether it is veto rights, consultation, or information.

Shared decisions have a nasty tendency not to be made by anyone. Avoid putting yourself in that scenario.

How to Manage the Process with Stakeholders

Up: You ask how major decisions are made.

Across: You negotiate how major decisions are made.

Down: You inform how major decisions are made.

It is not good enough to think you know how this process should play out or to assume that your stakeholders are on the same page with you on this. Make the effort to define the major decisions clearly and know how they will be made. Whether you make a decision that your boss thought was his or your direct report is making a decision that you felt was yours, it usually leads to uncomfortable circumstances at best and exploding land mines at worst. Make sure all the key players, especially your boss, view decision rights the same way.

That's the easy part. The trickier part is understanding where the real decision power resides. The three key sources of power are deciders (Who makes the decisions? Who sets the rules?), influencers, and implementers (Who controls the resources required to implement decisions?). It is important to consider how they interact and how they impact the organization when you are establishing your decision-making process.

Communication Preferences

Use these Fuzzy Front End prestart meetings to begin to understand stakeholders' communication preferences. Pay particular attention to mode, manner, frequency, and disagreements.

- Mode refers to the type of communication: e-mail, text, voice mail, in person, and so on.
- Manner is the style of communication: more formal and disciplined or less.
- Frequency is how often people prefer to be communicated with: daily updates, weekly, only when the project is completed, and so on.

You won't know others' preferences unless you ask. Do so.

Disagreements

Different people prefer being disagreed with in different ways, ranging from:

1. Never disagree with me.
2. Challenge me one-on-one, but only in private.

3. Challenge me in team meetings, but never let anyone outside "the family" know what you're thinking.
4. Challenge me in any meetings, but gently.
5. Gloves off, all the time, because public challenges communicate the culture we want.

Ask about this, but don't believe the initial answers you get. Initially, start at the top of the list, and wait to see how your key stakeholders, and especially your boss, respond to disagreements and challenges from others before you start disagreeing with them or challenging them.

5. Manage Your Personal and Office Setup

Step five of the Fuzzy Front End is to manage your personal and office setup well before Day One. No matter how much you try, you cannot give the new job your best efforts until you get comfortable about your family's setup. Taking the time to figure out housing, schools, transportation, and the like is not a luxury. It is a business imperative. The more drastic the move, the more issues you'll need to solve.

Similarly, make sure someone is getting your office set up before Day One. This doesn't have to be done perfectly because you can evolve as you go, though do make sure your office sends the right message about your approach: formal versus informal, functional versus welcoming.

There is no better time to get these resolved than during the Fuzzy Front End. If you wait, these things will distract you at a time when everyone is making those first and lasting impressions of your performance. Leverage the checklists at the end of this chapter to help get these done well before Day One.

Finally, make sure your human resources partner is accommodating your needs by helping you assimilate culturally and accelerate your plan, so you can ensure an impactful Day One. Tools 2.6 and 2.7 will help.

6. Plan Your Day One, Early Days, and First 100 Days

Step six of the Fuzzy Front End is to plan your Day One, early days, and first 100 days. There is a lot to learn in the Fuzzy Front End. The tools presented in this chapter will guide you along the way, but they are not designed to be all-inclusive. Instead, think of this process as a starting point for your entry into your new role. If you follow the process to this point, you will have completed a reasonably in-depth dive into your new organization's people, plans, practices, and purpose.

The knowledge gathered from your due diligence and your own self-study coupled with what you learn in your prestart conversations should enable you to begin to put things in context and help you figure out what you want to do on that first day, during that first week, and during those first 100 days. With this knowledge base, you can use Tool 2.1 at the end of this chapter to begin the outline of your 100-Day Plan. One of the most important choices you must make is how to engage the culture. So reconfirm that choice at the end of your Fuzzy Front End, just before you head into Day One.

The Fuzzy Front End approach detailed here will be effective in almost any scenario, no matter the role, function, or industry. Follow it and you'll be well on your way to better results faster. Some situations are unique enough to warrant slight enhancements or additional steps. Four circumstances where you might want to manage your Fuzzy Front End differently are:

1. Getting promoted from within
2. Leading a merger/acquisition
3. Leading a reorganization
4. Making an international move

There's more on each of these at www.onboardingtools.com.

Manage Getting Promoted from within Differently

Although the basics of this chapter apply to getting promoted from within or making a lateral transfer, there are some important differences:

You can't control the context—so prepare in advance; be ready to adjust as required. Understand the context (planned, unplanned, or interim). Secure the resources and support you need. Go with the flow, regain control of the situation, or jump into the dirty work as appropriate.

It's hard to make a clean break—so take control of your own message and transition. Manage the announcement cascade. Secure your base, ensuring your *old* area's ongoing success and recognizing the people who helped you along the way. Then use part of the time before you start to assess your predecessor's legacy, what you'll keep and change.

There is no honeymoon—so, set direction and generate momentum quickly after the start. Evolve the stated and de facto strategies. Improve operations and strengthen your organization.

Manage the Fuzzy Front End of a Merger/Acquisition Differently

The Fuzzy Front End concepts apply to all leadership transitions, with four points of emphasis for mergers and acquisitions, including the need to:

1. Develop an integration plan that delivers the deal objectives—whether it is deep functional integration or investment in innovation. Be flexible; there is no one approach to integration that will be appropriate in all situations. Keep the end in mind.

2. Choose which culture to merge into which (avoiding the generally doomed approach of trying to co-create a brand-new culture from scratch). At the same time, be proactive about specific elements of the acquired culture you wish to carry into your culture—integrations are unique moments to inject your culture with new ideas, new approaches, and new energy.

3. Perform an initial role sort before Day One to answer everyone's first question, "What does this mean for me?" See Tool 2.8.

4. Enroll the leadership teams in the change process, pulling them together to align on their goals, roles, responsibilities, reporting lines, decision rights, and governance, while co-creating a consistent message around the rationale for the merger and details about the change process. Doing this is a critical step toward unifying your new combined leadership team. See Tool 2.9.

Manage the Fuzzy Front End of a Reorganization/Restart Differently

This Fuzzy Front End approach also applies to reorganizations and restarts with a couple points of emphasis: There's an increased need to emphasize the platform for change—generally an external market driver to motivate people to take action in support of the change.

Second, there's a need for clarity around what parts of the culture are to stay and which will change. Figure it out and communicate it quickly to head off confusion and backtracking. Tool 2.10 will help you think through your announcement cascade.

Manage the Fuzzy Front End of an International Move Differently

The nice thing about switching countries is that no one (including you) expects you to know anything. You are completely, certifiably, consciously incompetent. Don't laugh. It's a privileged state that you want to leverage while you can. But, while doing so, you'll want to be making genuine efforts to adapt to the new culture.

- Get a head start and get help—with the move. Do not take a shortcut in the personal setup time, especially if you're moving your family. This is high-stress stuff.
- Get a head start—with the job. By definition, your learning curve is going to be steeper. So pay attention to your learning plan.
- Manage your message carefully, paying attention to both linguistic and cultural translations.
- Build the team while respecting individuals and their cultural heritage. Trying to impose your country's ways of behaving and relating, attitudes, values, and working environment on a different country's team members is almost certainly doomed to failure.
- Don't forget your colleagues back in your home country. You may need their assistance in leveraging help from headquarters to execute successfully in your new assignment.

HOT TIP

As long as you've shown respect for your host, cultural flubs are almost always overlooked and won't be damaging to you or the team. Sometimes, when handled properly they can help ease the transition or create a team bond. Be respectful. Make an honest effort to learn the culture. And apologize when you make a mistake.

Leverage the Fuzzy Front End: Summary and Implications

During the Fuzzy Front End, you should:

1. Determine your leadership approach given the context and culture you face.
2. Identify key stakeholders up, down, and across.
3. Craft your entry message using current best thinking.
4. Jump-start key relationships and accelerate your learning.
5. Manage your personal and office setup.
6. Plan your Day One, early days, and first 100 days.

Although this approach is generally applicable, there are some important differences in certain situations, such as getting promoted from within; managing a merger, acquisition, or reorganization; or making an international move.

QUESTIONS YOU SHOULD ASK YOURSELF

What is the organization's business context?

How ready is the culture to change?

Whom do I need to engage for support during this process?

Who are the likely contributors, detractors, and watchers?

Do I have the time I need before I start? (If not, can I create it?)

Have I optimized the time I've got?

Should I consider a different start date?

Am I being sufficiently clear about the changes?

Will everyone understand what the changes mean to them personally?

Is my new leadership team enrolled in the change?

What am I communicating during my Fuzzy Front End?

Do I understand my audience?

Have I leveraged what I know to craft my message?

Am I controlling my message?

Am I comfortable with my before Day One objectives?

Is my learning plan strong enough?

What other resources can help with my office and family setup?

Additional Articles and Tools on www.onboardingtools.com

2A.1   100-Day Worksheet Sample: New Company

2A.2   100-Day Worksheet Sample: Promoted from Within

2A.3   100-Day Worksheet Sample: Merging Teams

2A.4   100-Day Worksheet Sample: First-Time Leader

2A.5   100-Day Worksheet Sample: International

2A.6   100-Day Worksheet for the Next 100 days

2A.7   Stakeholder Map

100-Day Plan Worksheet*

Use this tool to capture foundational elements of your 100-Day Plan.

Job

Why you:

Why them:

Approach

Context:

Culture:

Risk profile:

ACES:

Stakeholders

Up (direct, indirect):

Across (internal, external):

Down (direct, indirect):

TOOL 2.1   100-Day Plan Worksheet (continued)

Message

Platform for change (*Why*):

Vision (*What*):

Call to action (*How*):

Headline:

Communication points:

Before Day One

Jump-start key relationships:

Jump-start learning:

Personal and office setup:

Day One/Early Days

Welcome:

(*continued*)

New Leader Assimilation:

Message in action:

Live meetings/Site visits:

Phone calls:

Tactical Capacity Building Blocks

Strategic:
Burning Imperative set by day 30
Date:
Method:

Operational:
Milestone Management in place by day 45
Date:
Method:

Early Wins jump-started by day 60
Date:
Method:

Organizational:
Team roles set by day 70
Date:
Method:

Ongoing:
Communication/Leadership Protocols in place (day/week/month/ quarter/year) by day 100
Date:
Method:

TOOL 2.2
Context Assessment*

Use this tool as a guideline to assessing the business environment, the organizational history, and the recent business performance.

Business Environment

Customers

low satisfaction ......|......|......|......|......|...... highly satisfied

Collaborators

combative ......|......|......|......|......|...... supportive

Capabilities

lagging industry ......|......|......|......|......|...... leading industry

Competitors

ahead of us ......|......|......|......|......|...... behind us

Conditions

unfavorable ......|......|......|......|......|...... favorable

(continued)

TOOL 2.2   Context Assessment (continued)

Organizational History

Founder's intent:

Organizational heroes:

Guiding stories and myths:

Recent Business Performance

Absolute and relative results:

Recent trends:

Positive drivers:

Negative drivers:

Need to change:

less urgent   ......|......|......|......|......|......   urgent

TOOL 2.3

ACES Context/Culture Map[*]

Use this tool (Figure 2.1) to map the organization's *need* and *readiness* to change and thus your approach.

FIGURE 2.1   Context and Culture

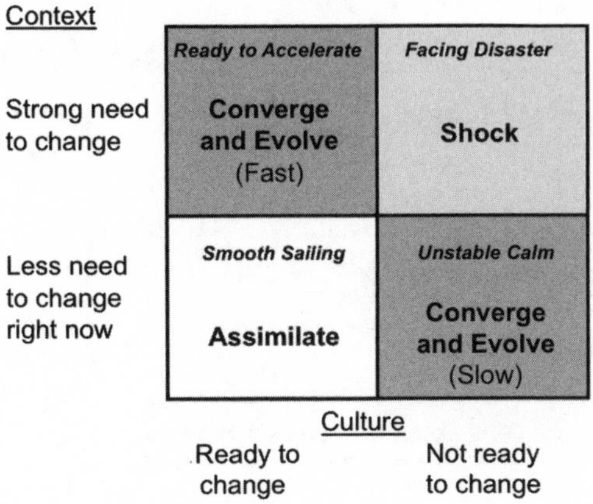

Context

	Ready to Accelerate	Facing Disaster
Strong need to change	**Converge and Evolve** (Fast)	**Shock**
Less need to change right now	*Smooth Sailing* **Assimilate**	*Unstable Calm* **Converge and Evolve** (Slow)

Culture

Ready to change	Not ready to change

---

[*]Copyright © PrimeGenesis LLC. To customize this document, download Tool 2.3 from www.onboardingtools.com. The document can be opened, edited, and printed.

TOOL 2.4

Communication Planning*

FIGURE 2.3   Communication Plan

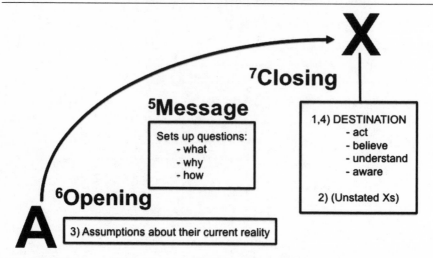

Use the process shown in Figure 2.3 to help you craft and manage your message.

1. Identify your destination.

   What is the desired reaction and behavior you want from your audience/constituents?

   What specifically do you want or not want them to understand, believe, say about you, or do?

2. Be explicit about unstated Xs. What do you want listeners to think about you?

3. Assess current reality.

   What does your audience/constituency currently understand, believe, or say about you? Why?

---

*Copyright © PrimeGenesis LLC. To customize this document, download Tool 2.4 from www.onboardingtools.com. The document can be opened, edited, and printed.

TOOL 2.4   Communication Planning (continued)

Develop a risk management plan, including potential obstacles, negative rumors, sabotage, legal requirements, unintended consequences, and scenarios.

4. Reevaluate destination in light of assumptions about audience.

5. Bridge the gap.

What do people need to be aware of, understand, and believe to move from current reality to your destination?

6. Develop core messages and key communication points (maximum five core messages).

7. Package the message.

How should core messages be packaged for optimum effectiveness?

What kind of supporting data do you need?

What is your key opening message?

What is your key closing message?

8. Deliver the message.

What are the best vehicles to reach your audience or constituents? What is the optimum combination? What is the best timing to release the message? Who and what influences whom?

How do you best plant the follow-up seeds?

9. Evolve.

How should you modify your message based on what you've learned from your conversations and interactions with others?

TOOL 2.5

Onboarding Conversation Framework[*]

Use this tool as a guideline to structure your onboarding conversations.

Key questions to ask during onboarding conversations (in addition to all the questions you would normally ask):

1. Learning

    What is your read on the general situation?

    What strengths/capabilities are required?

    Which strengths/capabilities exist now? Examples?

2. Expectations

    What do you see as key priorities? Lower priorities? Current untouchables?

    What resources are available to invest against these priorities?

3. Implementation

    Tell me about the control points (metrics and process: meetings, reports)

    Tell me about some of the key decisions we make. Who makes them? How?

What Decision	1. A on Own	2. A with B's Input	3. Shared	4. B with A's Input	5. B on Own

What is the best way to communicate with you? (Mode/manner/ frequency/disagreements?)

[*] Copyright © PrimeGenesis LLC. To customize this document, download Tool 2.5 from www.onboardingtools.com. The document can be opened, edited, and printed.

TOOL 2.6
Personal Set-Up Relocation Checklist*

Use this tool as a time-based checklist to help manage your move when relocating.

ASAP

☐ Get set up: create move file, post calendar, and so on.

☐ Choose a moving company. Get multiple bids and references.

☐ Research schools at destination. Public? Independent?

☐ Start to gather children's essential records in a secure folder that travels with you.

☐ Choose a real estate agent at destination.

☐ Make arrangements to sell or rent your current home.

☐ Secure travel documents (passports, visas) and make travel arrangements for family and pets.

☐ Research temporary housing options in case they become necessary.

☐ Look hard at your possessions for things to give away or sell.

☐ Start a log of moving expenses for employer or taxes.

☐ Start to gather information about resources in destination city.

One Month Before Moving Day

☐ Fill out change of address forms (for Internal Revenue Service, subscriptions and bills, etc.).

☐ Obtain medical and dental records, X-rays, and prescription histories.

☐ Set up a checking account and safe-deposit box in your new city/country.

(continued)

TOOL 2.6   Personal Set-Up Relocation Checklist (continued)

☐ Take inventory of your belongings before they are packed, ideally with pictures.

☐ Arrange for help on moving day, especially looking after children.

Two Weeks Before Moving Day

☐ Confirm travel reservations.

☐ Clean rugs and clothing and have them wrapped for moving.

☐ Close bank accounts and have your funds wired to your new bank.

☐ Check with your insurance agent to ensure coverage through your homeowner's or renter's policy during the move.

☐ Give a close friend or relative your travel route and schedule.

One Week Before Moving Day

☐ Switch utility services to new address.

☐ Prearrange for important services—such as a working phone.

☐ Collect valuables (important documents, jewelry, etc.) from safe-deposit boxes, and so on.

On Move-Out Day

☐ Be sure valuables are secure and ready to go with you. Carry important documents, currency, and jewelry yourself, or use registered mail.

☐ If customary, have cash on hand to tip movers.

☐ Have water, drinks, and snacks available for movers in appropriate place.

TOOL 2.6   Personal Set-Up Relocation Checklist (continued)

On Move-In Day

☐ Have phone/camera on hand to record damages.

☐ Have people ready to (1) check in items and (2) direct items to right place.

☐ Have water, drinks, and snacks available for movers in appropriate place.

TOOL 2.7
Office Set-Up Checklist*

Use this checklist to address office setup issues *before* Day One.

☐ Office (whose) or place to work

☐ Desk

☐ Chair

☐ Office attitude (imposing and formal vs. welcoming and informal)

☐ Visitor chairs

☐ Couches

☐ Tables

☐ Cabinets

☐ Whiteboards

☐ Flip charts

☐ Audiovisual

☐ Employee number

☐ Security pass

☐ Keys

☐ Parking

☐ Personal computer

☐ Laptop

☐ E-mail/system access

☐ Phones/voice mail access

☐ Cell phones

☐ Stationery

TOOL 2.7   Office Set-Up Checklist (continued)

☐ Files

☐ Business cards

☐ Travel profile

☐ Support

☐ Executive assistant

☐ Other

TOOL 2.8
Leadership Team Role Sort*

Use this tool to do an initial role sort

	Current	**Current**	**New**	
Role	Team A	Team B	Combined Team	Path for Person Not on New Team

---

Leadership Team Pre-Start Alignment Session[*]

Use this tool as a guideline for crafting your prestart alignment session.

Objective

Clarity on Day One communications: who, what, when, how, and why
Most often focused on three items:

1. Rationale for the merger—benefits for customers and internally

2. What it means for each person on Day One (reporting, roles, responsibilities) and acknowledgement that could change over time

3. Communication pace and protocol during the change process

Benefits

Clarity and alignment on messaging
Sense of being in the know for acquired leadership team members
Beginning of team building because the combined leadership teams have co-created the message

Prep

Acquiring leader thinks through going-in hypotheses regarding messaging

Acquiring leader briefs and collaborates with acquired leader on meeting objective and flow

(continued)

TOOL 2.9   Leadership Team Pre-Start Alignment Session (continued)

Welcome

Leader welcomes group, restates objective (clarity on Day One communication)

Acquired leader or others remind people what has happened, what is set

Facilitator intro (agenda, expectations, around-the-table intros)

Working hypothesis

Leader or others lay out entry messaging and plan (who saying what to whom when, how, and why)

Discussion

Group input into entry messaging and plan

Converge

Agree on messaging and plan

Actions

Clarify details of plan for Day One

Next steps for this group after Day One and meeting review

Announcement Cascade*

Use this tool to plan your announcement cascade.

1. **Stakeholders** (internal and external)

    Emotionally impacted:

    Directly impacted:

    Indirectly impacted:

    Less impacted:

2. **Message**

    Platform for change:

    Headline:

    Vision:

    Message points:

    Call to action:

(*continued*)

---

*Copyright © PrimeGenesis LLC. To customize this document, download Tool 2.10 from www.onboardingtools.com. The document can be opened, edited, and printed.

TOOL 2.10   Announcement Cascade (continued)

3. **Preannouncement Timeline** (one-on-ones, small groups, large groups, before announcement day)

     One-on-One:

     Announcement day

     One-on-One:

     Small Groups:

4. **Formal Announcement**

     Method:

     Timing:

5. **Postannouncement Timeline** (one-on-ones, small groups, large groups, mass)

     One-on-one:

     Small groups:

     Large groups:

CHAPTER 3

Take Control of Day One

MAKE A POWERFUL FIRST IMPRESSION.
CONFIRM YOUR ENTRY MESSAGE.

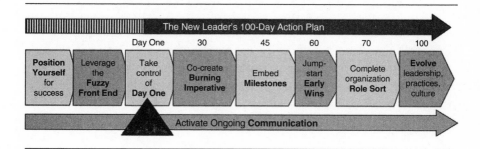

Our brains remember information "presented first and last, and have an inclination to forget the middle items."[1] People will remember vividly their first impressions of you and their last interaction with you. Although you can update their last interaction constantly, you are going to be stuck with those first impressions. So, be careful when choosing them. Be careful about the messages you send with your words, with your actions, with the order of your actions, and with the signs and symbols you deploy.

This is why Day One is such a meaningful pivot point for onboarding. Many people who are important to your new role will form their

---

[1] Elizabeth Hilton, 2001, "Differences in Visual and Auditory Short-Term Memory," *Indiana University South Bend Journal* 4.

first, indelible impression of you on this day. As with the Fuzzy Front End, reconnect with your own behavior, relationship, attitude, value, and environment (BRAVE) preferences and orientation, and think carefully about whom you are encountering and already starting to influence.

There is no one right way to do this, but there are many wrong ways to do this. It is all about the first impression received. Different people will have different impressions of the same thing depending on their perspective and filters. The problem is that before your first interactions with them, you can't understand their perspective and filters. So not only is there no one right answer, but it will also be difficult to figure out the best answer for your particular situation.

This is another reason it is so valuable to get a jump start on relationships and learning during the Fuzzy Front End. One of the powerful things about embracing the Fuzzy Front End is that it enables you to manage the initial impressions you make on those key people outside the noise of Day One. Managed well, it will also help you make better choices about your early days.

What Are You Going to Do on Day One?

That question, more than any other, stumps our clients. Most leaders fail to think about and plan Day One as thoroughly as it deserves. In fact, even those leaders who do a phenomenal job throughout the Fuzzy Front End find themselves stumbling on their first day. For some reason, leaders are often lulled into complacency when deciding what to do on Day One. Often they passively accept a schedule that someone else has planned out for them. Or they plan to do what seems to be the traditional Day One activities of meeting those people around their office or filling out the required forms, unpacking, and setting up their office.

Not you. What you say and do on Day One is going to inspire others. Not with cheesy motivational tactics, but through meaningful words and actions that create excitement about the things to come. Do not underestimate Day One's importance. Plan it with great care and make sure it communicates your message, exactly as you want it, to the people you most need to reach.

No two leaders' first days will ever be the same because the combination of variables in every situation begs for different Day

One plans. However, when planning your Day One, here are some general guidelines and principles to consider:

It is personal. As a leader, you impact people's lives. These people will try hard to figure out you and your potential impact as soon as they can. They may even rush to judgment. Keep that in mind at all times.

Order counts. Be circumspect about the order in which you meet with people and the timing of when you do what throughout Day One and your early days.

Messages matter. Have a message. Know what you are going to say and not say. Have a bias toward listening. Know that strong opinions, long-winded introductions, and efforts to prove yourself immediately are rarely, if ever, good Day One tactics. People will be looking to form opinions early. Keep that in mind while deciding when to listen, when to share, what to ask, whom to ask, and how you answer. When you speak, keep it brief, on point, and meaningful.

Location counts. Think about where you will show up for work on Day One. Do not just show up at your designated office by default.

Signs and symbols count. Be aware of all the ways in which you communicate, well beyond just words. Think BRAVE!

Timing counts. Day One does not have to match the first day you get paid. Decide which day you want to communicate as Day One to facilitate other choices about order and location.

Tool 3.1 at the end of the chapter provides a convenient checklist for thinking about these things.

The Sierra Club's executive director Michael Brune did a particularly good job of managing his Day One. He thought through his message in advance and then communicated it live, face-to-face, and via social media on his first day so that everyone would know what was on his mind. He smartly used several communication methods to reach a wide range of people in their own preferred ways of communication.

Owning Day One

As Brune explained in a phone interview, he took time out before he started to research the organization's history and think through what he wanted to get done on the first day, first week, and first month.

"Since I knew I was going to go deep . . . I wanted to have a couple of big priorities that I wanted to stick to for the first month. . . . Having those touchstones helped me to bring a little bit of order into the chaos of starting a new job."

Those touchstones included:

1. Being more solutions oriented. *"For years we'd been good at stopping (bad) things."* Now it seemed to be important to help move good things forward in *"symbolic and substantive ways."*
2. Identifying the bottom lines.—Agree on the things that we (the Sierra Club) could not compromise on as a way to provide a backstop beyond which we could not go.
3. Modernizing the Club, using technology and polishing the brand to be more energetic.

On his first day, Brune wrote in his blog:

Today's my first day. I'm inspired and honored to be a part of such a democratically-governed, volunteer-powered organization. From helping to protect Yosemite and millions of acres of wilderness to the more recent work of building powerful alliances with labor and impacted communities, Sierra Club volunteers and staff have played a pivotal role in many of the most important environmental victories over the past century.

But as effective as the organization has been over the past 118 years, we need to do our best work in the years ahead. The challenges— and opportunities—are too great.

Brune did several things right:

- He switched his identity and allegiance instantly, talking about himself as part of his new organization.
- He credited his predecessors and current team, telling people he hoped to follow their examples and build on their "victories."
- He started driving his message and communication points with what he said and what he did, wearing his own passion for the environment on his sleeve.
- He started by listening instead of talking, pontificating, or declaring. His first morning he met with his executive team to get an update on what they were doing and connect with work they'd already done. He learned where they thought the organization was strong and where they thought it needed help.

- Then, after listening to the executive team and taking that in, he had an all-staff, multioffice meeting to introduce himself to all and lay out his own initial observations about places needing attention.[2]

Make Careful Choices about Your Day One Plan

Using the preceding guidelines and your knowledge gained during your Fuzzy Front End, you should be well positioned to start planning how your Day One should take shape. Look for indications of what actions might be especially effective and powerful, and work those items into your agenda, if possible.

Many have found value in holding early meetings with as many of the people in their reporting line as they can muster—in person, by videoconference, by teleconference, or the like. These early meetings give all a chance to lay their eyes on you. It does not really matter what you say in these meetings because no one will remember much beyond hello unless you make a mistake. If they do remember, they'll probably remember the things you wish you'd never said. So, new leaders should say, "Hello, nice to be here," and not much else at this point.

Another valuable tool is the New Leader Assimilation Session. There is a template for this at the end of this chapter (Tool 3.2). It is easy to deploy and effective in bringing out all the questions that everyone really wants to ask in a forum where a critical mass can hear what you have to say, all at the same time. This prevents person A from filtering the message to person B, who filters it again, and so on.

There will always be rumors. But this process, originally created by Lynn Ulrich of the Wilfred Jarvis Institute and deployed in great depth at General Electric (GE), goes a long way toward squelching most of the rumors, innuendos, and misinformation. Hence, do this as early in your tenure as possible, preferably Day One. The session works in multiple scenarios, including new leaders entering new roles, as well as for new owners in the early days following an acquisition or a new investment by a private equity firm.

---

[2] George Bradt, 2011, "Powerful First Impressions: Michael Brune's Day One at the Sierra Club," *Forbes*, March 2.

You can be creative with this tool, in the event it is not practical to gather all team members in the same location. Martha, whose over-arching objective in her new role was to knit together a dispersed team—scattered across 12 states—into a cohesive unit, kicked off her Day One with an *all-hands* conference call, providing some information and laying out a virtual new leader assimilation process. Everyone was invited to send in comments and questions via e-mail over the next three days. Martha held another all-hands call on Day Four to address the issues. She followed up with regular updates, accomplishing her early goal of getting the entire team on the same page with regard to her objective and approach.

Don't Reinvent the Wheel:
Start with This Prototypical Agenda

Although no two executives' Day Ones are ever the same, it's often easier to start with a model.

You can use the following sample agenda as a guideline for crafting your own Day One:

Early-morning meeting with your boss to reconfirm and update.

Meet and greet over coffee, juice, or the like with broad group to say hello (and not much more).

One-on-one meetings as appropriate.

New Leader's Assimilation (Tool 3.2) with direct reports and their direct reports.

Afternoon activity/meetings/walkabout to reinforce key message.

End-of-day cocktails/coffee/social for more informal greetings.

Courtesy notes, voice mail for thank-you or follow-up, where needed and appropriate.

Brief communication with your boss or board member to begin the habit of staying connected, as appropriate.

Perhaps the best way to get across the power of a well-planned Day One is through examples of others' Day One experiences.

Leverage Your Agenda as a Symbol of What's Important

Edgar was joining a company as chief executive officer (CEO). The most important thing he had to do was to change the mind-set of the organization to become more customer focused.

"What are you doing Day One?"

"I've got this planned. I'm showing up, introducing myself to the team, and launching five committees to tackle the five most important priorities."

"What happened to being more customer focused?"

"What do you mean?"

"How does your planned Day One demonstrate that your main goal is to become more customer focused?"

"I guess it doesn't."

"What does it say to your customers?"

"Well, nothing, they won't know about it."

"Exactly."

Edgar changed his plans. He did introduce himself to the team, but then explained, "I'm leaving now. Because, before I'm prepared to talk to any of you about anything, I want to get out and spend some time with our customers."

Edgar then proceeded to talk to customers . . . for the next 10 days. On the third day, the chairman called him to express his concern. "What are you doing traipsing around the country? I hired you to run the business."

"I can't do that until I've learned a little about our customers."

By the end of the first week, customers started calling the chairman to tell him how impressed they were with the new CEO. "He listens. We're excited about him."

Finally, Edgar came back into the company with a comprehensive understanding of what the customers wanted and knowledge of where his company was falling short. He shared that knowledge with his new team. He met with his direct reports one-on-one to get their perspective on the customers and then used all that information to craft a Burning Imperative around a customer-centric vision.

He took the message forward by calling the top 50 leaders together to tell them how the new company Burning Imperative was crafted with their input as well as the customers'. He explained how the Burning Imperative drove the priorities. He said,

"Based on our jointly developed Burning Imperative, I'm happy to announce the formation of five committees to work on our top five priorities."

Although the top five priorities were essentially the same as he'd originally planned, they contained powerful nuances that better fit the customers' needs, and the initiatives had significantly more credibility because he involved the customers and his staff. His early actions sent a strong communication about the customer's role in the company going forward.

Choose Location, Signs, and Symbols with Care: People Will Notice

Thomas lived in Singapore and joined a large bank as head of its Asia group. He was going to work out of the Singapore office for a few months and then move to its Asia headquarters in Tokyo.

"What are you going to do on Day One?"

"I thought I'd go into the office, do paperwork, and start meeting people."

"Which office?"

"Singapore."

"Why?"

"Because I'm here. Why not?"

"Because you're the head of Asia and the Asian headquarters is Tokyo. If you start in Singapore, you'll be perceived as the head of the Singapore branch until you show up in Tokyo in January."

So, instead of starting in Singapore and doing paperwork, Thomas and his wife flew up to Tokyo and took his direct reports and their spouses out to dinner the night before he started. Then, at 9:00 AM Tokyo time, Thomas arranged a videoconference and introduced himself to his 256 regional employees while standing in the middle of the Tokyo trading floor. Then he met with direct reports during the day. Finally, to cap off his first day, he took the bank's largest customer in Japan out for dinner.

Do you see how these actions represent a big difference in terms of location, signs, and symbols? Everything communicates. Showing up to do paperwork in Singapore sends a different message from showing up and taking charge at the headquarters.

Don't Necessarily Go to Where Your Boss Is

Gerry was starting work in London, but most of his direct reports were in a newly acquired company in Birmingham. During his Fuzzy Front End, Gerry learned that the Birmingham folks were concerned that they would be required to move to London because of the merger. That wasn't the case, but Gerry realized that it could become a crippling fear. So he chose to spend Day One in Birmingham to ease people's fears and to address the rumors up front. He used the New Leader's Assimilation tool to extract the common fears of the Birmingham group and went in with a strong and credible message that their jobs and their location were safe. To further underscore the message, he set up an office that was complete and functional and hired a secretary at the Birmingham office before his Day One meetings.

On the other hand, Khalil was coming in to run three divisions of a different company. The largest was in Odessa near where he lived. The second largest was in Omaha, and the smallest was in Lawrence. His boss's office was in Lawrence. Khalil chose to spend Day One in Lawrence, attending his boss's staff meeting in the morning and then spending the afternoon with the division that reported to him. For Khalil, it was important to signal to his boss that, even though he was living in Odessa, he was going to be available to be part of his boss's team.

Leverage Your Message on Day One

Karen was coming into a bank to merge three divisions into one.

"How are you going to get to know the people at each division?"

"I'm in luck. Each division manager has an off-site meeting already planned for my first two weeks. I'm going to use those as a chance to meet the key players and get to know them."

"Will that be the first time you meet them?"

"Sure, why not?"

"Because it doesn't match with your main objective or your message."

The problem was that Karen's individual divisional meetings perpetuated the culture of three different divisions as opposed to one combined group. Each of the divisions was in proximity to each other. So to set a new course Karen rented a theater for Day One and invited the entire staff across all the old divisions. Then she introduced herself to the entire staff of the new division at the same time. She followed this with a social event designed to get the three divisions mingling.

She eventually went to the old divisions' off-sites, but only after setting the stage for the new combined division.

Be Present

Kim was coming into a new company as CEO. The old CEO and founder was going to stay on as chief innovation officer.

"Tell me about Day One."

"Oh, I'm all set. I am going to get in early to get my office set up. Then I am meeting with the old CEO from 9:00 to 11:00. Then meeting with the CFO [chief financial officer] from 11:00 to 12:00. After lunch I'm going to take care of some logistics and work on my messaging for my first official communication with the company."

"Are you a hermit?"

"What a silly question. Of course not."

"Well, if I work for you and if I haven't seen you by noon of your first day I'm pretty convinced you're either a hermit, or shy, or are not too concerned about 'us' since all you've done is lock yourself in your office."

Instead, Kim called a meeting of the company's top 100 managers at 8:30. She introduced herself, told everyone how glad she was to be there. She then had meetings with the old CEO and CFO. But, at this point, it was okay because she'd made an initial connection with her team.

Be Mindful of the Unintended Consequences

Arthur was moving from California to Montana to head up human resources at a large corporation. When asked what he was doing Day One, he suggested he was going to spend it in a human resources orientation. Most companies' human resource orientations are not something a senior executive should do on Day One. Almost always, that is best done during the Fuzzy Front End. But since Arthur was coming in to head human resources (HR), this was different. He needed to be there.

In the end, Arthur pushed back his official Day One so that he could go up to Montana a week early. He used that created time to meet with most of his key stakeholders. On his official Day One, he sat through every minute of the HR orientation, allowing no interruptions. It sent a message to his team that HR was indeed important, and it allowed him to have an informed opinion of the orientation process and how it needed to change.

At the end of his Day One, Arthur bumped into the CEO, who asked him how things were going so far. Arthur told him about the premeetings with peers and his teams as well as his positive impressions of the HR orientation. The CEO could not figure out how Arthur had gotten all that done in just one day.

Dress to Fit In

Victor got invited to a meeting at a golf club on a Saturday morning. He was told that the dress was business casual. But he was in Japan, so he suspected that might mean something a little different. He wore gray flannels, a formal shirt, and a blazer. As it turned out, he was the only one not in a suit and tie.

Conversely, Dave joined a company where people dressed casually—jeans, shorts, flip-flops, T-shirts—even to the most formal meetings. He noticed the casual clothes during his Fuzzy Front End, but still decided to show up in a suit on Day One because he thought it signified leadership. After two months, he was still wearing a suit to work. No tie, but the suit trousers and jacket. People thought he was clinging to the armor of his old ways and that he was turned off or disapproving of the new culture. His direct reports even referred to him as "The Suit." He should have lost the suit before Day One.

Think carefully about Day One. Think about how you want to learn and communicate. Do you want to start by meeting your team in the office or off-site? Should your meetings be structured as one-on-ones or as a group? Do you want to start with a full-company meeting? Do you want to start with casual meetings? Do you want to start with the team or with customers? From the preceding examples, you can deduce that there is no one right answer. But just by asking yourself the questions and answering thoughtfully, you will be miles ahead of the game.

What Not to Do on Day One

Don't leave to look for an apartment or home.

Don't show up late.

Don't have lunch meetings with former colleagues.

Don't consume alcohol at lunch.

Don't tell anything but the mildest joke.

Don't spend excessive time on the phone setting up logistics for your move.

Don't dress inappropriately.

Don't decorate your office.

Don't say anything (good or bad) about your former company.

Don't say anything negative about anybody in your new company.

Don't use a PowerPoint presentation to introduce yourself.

Don't schedule a doctor's appointment.

Don't tell too much information about your personal life.

Don't panic if things go awry.

HOT TIP

Manage Day One: Even though everything communicates, some communication is more important than others. How you spend Day One leaves an indelible impression. Control the agenda, even if you have to redefine which day is Day One.

HOT TIP

Day One is a critical part of *assimilation*. Welcome and get help from HR in terms of getting started working with others. Assimilation is a big deal. Doing it well makes things far easier. Getting it wrong triggers relationship risks. There are a couple of things beyond basic orientation that can make a huge difference. Encourage HR or others to set up onboarding conversations for you with members of your formal and informal/shadow networks. Ask HR or others to do periodic check-ins with those networks. If there are issues, you want to know about them early, so you can adjust.

Take Control of Day One: Summary and Implications

At the start of a new role, everything is magnified. Thus it is critical to be particularly thoughtful about everything you do and say and don't do and don't say—and what order you do or say them in.

As you plan your own Day One, here are a couple of things to keep in mind:

- *It is personal.* As a leader, you impact people's lives. Those people will try very hard to figure out you and your potential impact as soon as they can. They may even rush to judgment. Keep that in mind at all times.

- *Order counts.* Be circumspect about the order in which you meet with people and the timing of when you do what throughout Day One and your early days.

- *Messages matter.* Have a message. Know what you are going to say and not say. Have a bias toward listening. Know that strong opinions, long-winded introductions, and efforts to prove yourself immediately are rarely, if ever, good Day One tactics. People will be looking to form opinions early. Keep that in mind while deciding when to listen, when to share, what to ask, whom to ask, and how you answer. When speaking keep it brief, on point, and meaningful.

- *Location counts.* Think about where you will show up for work on Day One. Do not just show up at your designated office by default.

- *Signs and symbols count.* Be aware of all the ways in which you communicate, well beyond just words.

- *Timing counts.* Day One does not have to match the first day you get paid. Decide which day you want to communicate as Day One to facilitate other choices about order and location.

QUESTIONS YOU SHOULD ASK YOURSELF

What am I doing on Day One? What does it communicate?

Am I being thoughtful about all the ways I am communicating on Day One?

Am I making the impression I want to make on the people I choose to make it on?

What might people want to know, and how will I answer the questions should I be asked?

What is my message and does my Day One agenda support it?

TOOL 3.1
Day One Checklist*

Use the format below to plan your Day One.

Official Day One

_____

_____

Effective Day One

_____

_____

Your Message_____

_____

Your Entry Plan (detailed, calendared)

Initial Large-Group Meetings

_____

_____

Initial Small-Group Meetings

_____

_____

New Leader Assimilation Date?

_____

_____

Other Internal Stakeholder Meetings

_____

_____

External Stakeholder Meetings

_____

_____

(continued)

TOOL 3.1   Day One Checklist (continued)

External Stakeholder Phone Calls

_____

_____

Meals—Breakfast, Lunch, Dinner

_____

_____

Walking around Time

_____

_____

End-of-Day Thank-Yous

_____

_____

_____

TOOL 3.2
New Leader Assimilation[*]

The Ulrich/GE new leader assimilation process gets questions on the table and resolved immediately that would fester without it. This is a useful session to conduct in the first days or weeks of a new leadership role.

STEP 1: Provide a brief introduction and an overview of the objectives of the session, and review the process to all involved (team and new leader).

STEP 2: Team members, without the new leader present, generate questions about:

1. The new leader (you).

   (Questions may concern professional profile or personal hopes, dreams, rumors, preconceptions, concerns, etc.)

2. The new leader as a team leader.

   (Questions may concern what the leader knows about the team, priorities, work style, norms, communication, rumors, etc.)

3. The new leader as a member of the broader organization.

   (Questions may concern what the leader knows about the organization, how he or she fits, priorities, assumptions, expectations, rumors, etc.)

   The team should also answer the following questions that they'll present to the new leader.

4. What does the new leader need to know to be successful in the new role?

   What are the top three issues?

   What are the secrets to being effective?

   Are there any ideas for the new leader?

(continued)

---

[*] Copyright © PrimeGenesis LLC. To customize this document, download Tool 3.2 from www.onboardingtools.com. The document can be opened, edited, and printed.

TOOL 3.2   New Leader Assimilation (continued)

5. What significant issues need to be addressed immediately?

   Are there any quick fixes that are needed now?

   Are there any difficult areas of the business that the new leader should know about?

6. Other questions and ideas?

   What is the one question that you are afraid to ask?

   What additional messages do you have?

STEP 3: New leader rejoins team to answer questions, listen, and learn.

TOOL 3.3
New Owner Assimilation*

This is a slight adaptation of the Ulrich/GE new leader assimilation process to get questions on the table and resolved immediately that would fester without it in the early days of an acquisition, as well as after a new platform investment by a private equity firm.

STEP 1: Provide a brief introduction and an overview of the objectives of the session, and review the process to all involved (team and new owner).

STEP 2: Team members, without the new owner present, generate questions about:

1. The new owner (you).

    (Questions may concern professional profile or history or personal hopes, dreams, rumors, preconceptions, concerns, etc.)

2. The new owner as a team leader.

    (Questions may concern what the leader knows about the team, current priorities, work style, norms, communication, rumors, etc.)

3. The new owner as owner.

    (Questions may concern what the owner knows about the organization, how team members will fit with the new owner's vision, priorities, assumptions, expectations, rumors, etc.)

    The team should also answer the following questions that they'll present to the new owner:

4. What does the new owner need to know to avoid missteps?

    What are the top three issues?

    What are the secrets to being effective?

    Are there any ideas for the new owner?

(continued)

---

* Copyright © PrimeGenesis LLC. To customize this document, download Tool 3.3 from www.onboardingtools.com. The document can be opened, edited, and printed.

TOOL 3.3   New Owner Assimilation (continued)

---

5. What significant issues need to be addressed immediately?

    Are there any quick fixes that are needed now?

    Are there any difficult areas of the business that the new owner should know about?

6. Other questions and ideas?

    What is the one question that you are afraid to ask?

    What additional messages do you have?

STEP 3: New owner rejoins team to answer questions, listen, and learn.

STEP 4: Separately, the new owner meets with management on matters of reporting and governance.

1. What is expected in terms of financial and key initiative reporting (frequency, data, ownership)?

2. Who has responsibility for various aspects of reporting and analysis (CFO, private equity owner)?

3. What is the protocol for communication (what gets reported, how quickly, by whom, and to whom)?

4. How will decisions be made (for each type, who is responsible, accountable, informed, consulted)?

CHAPTER 4

Activate Ongoing Communication

ESTABLISH LEADERSHIP AND
BEGIN CULTURAL TRANSFORMATION.

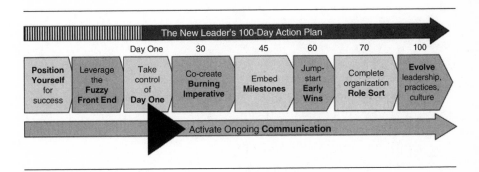

Everything communicates. Everything. Even the things you don't do and don't say send powerful signals to everybody in the organization observing you.

Because we live in the midst of a communication revolution, the guidelines for communicating are changing dramatically. As much as you would like to treat communication as a logical, sequential, ongoing communication campaign, in many cases, you must manage it as an iterative set of concurrent conversations.

The prescription for communication during the time between Day One and co-creating a Burning Imperative is counterintuitive and stressful for new leaders following this program. The fundamental approach is to converge and evolve. The time before co-creating a Burning Imperative is all about converging. This means you can't launch your full-blown communication efforts yet. You can't stand up and tell people your new ideas. If you do, they are your ideas, not invented here and not the team's ideas. So this period leading up to co-creating a Burning Imperative is marked by a lot of listening and learning. Your learning will be directed by your message. You'll be living your message, but you're most definitely not launching a communication campaign of any sort. (This is one of those things that you don't do that will communicate volumes to all your observers.) Keep that in mind as you go through the rest of this chapter, which lays out some points on communication that you may or may not start during this period, but will use later.

Where to Start and What You Need to Know

Before activating your ongoing communication efforts after Day One, you'll need to address several key components, each of which is essential. As a foundation to your approach, per Chapter 2 and before launch you should have done the following:

1. Identified Your *Target Audience*
2. Crafted an *Overarching Message*
3. Determined the *Key Communication Points*

This is a good time to take a stop and rethink each of these elements given what you have learned and make any adjustments so they accurately reflect your current best thinking.

Use Your Communication to Drive Engagement

There's an ever-strengthening body of evidence that engaged employees produce better results.[1] Engagement is too important and dynamic a metric to live with a binary distinction between the engaged and unengaged. Instead, think of engagement in terms of four levels: committed, contributors, compliant, and disengaged.

---

[1] Steve Crabtree, 2013, "Worldwide, 13% of Employees Are Engaged at Work," Gallup, October 8.

Committed: The committed are driven by the purpose, the cause, and doing good for others. They believe and will do whatever it takes to accomplish the desired results. Keep them committed with communication that touches their emotions and gets them to believe viscerally in what you're trying to do together.

Contributors: The contributors are good at what they do and it shows. They enjoy their work and their output is positive and helps keep moving the ball up the field. They are important players, but not necessarily leaders. Communicate with them directly so they understand what is required of them.

Compliant: The compliant are primarily driven by what is good for them and concerned about their basic needs. Compliant people aren't hurting the organization, but they are not primary drivers of change. They are doing what they are told and no more. These are your watchers and will probably stay watchers. The goal is to make them aware of what they need to do and make sure it gets done.

Disengaged: The disengaged have checked out emotionally. They don't believe in the platform for change, the vision, or the call to action. They won't do what the organization needs them to do. Their complete disconnect qualifies them as detractors. If they don't immediately respond to the new messaging, move them out, quickly.

Hold that thought for a moment.

Consider What Drives Happiness

People on your team want to be happy. Everyone finds happiness by some combination of:

1. Doing good for others
2. Doing things they are good at
3. Doing good for themselves

In the work environment, the committed are motivated by all three elements and therefore are usually among the happiest team members. The contributors are motivated by elements two and three, and the compliant are motivated by element three. Sadly, the disengaged are not finding happiness in any element.

Different people are motivated more by one bucket than by another. The more focused someone is on doing good for others, the more likely that the other elements of happiness fall into place as well. Mother Theresa was almost exclusively focused on doing good for others; but, while she did that, she also became very good at what she did, and her work was good for her. Great artists, such as cellist Yo-Yo Ma, may not care about the impact they make on others or their own rewards; they just want to pursue their art for the sake of the art, because it brings them joy to do what they are good at. Some Hollywood producers and actors are driven more by doing what's good for themselves, money, and fame, rather than the quality of the films they create.

Add that thought to the thought you're holding on engagement.

Maslow's Needs

The core of Maslow's theory is that there is a hierarchy of needs.[2] At the bottom people must satisfy their physiological and safety needs. With those in place, they can move on to belonging and esteem. Then, ultimately they can tackle needs for self-actualization.

Add Maslow's hierarchy to the happiness and engagement thoughts you're holding, mix in a little communication planning, and out pops a framework to bridge from communication approaches to engagement levels (see Table 4.1).

Table 4.1
Communication Engagement Levels

Needs (Maslow)	Happiness Driver	Communication Approach	Communication Result	Engagement Level
Self-actualization	Good for others	Emotional	Belief	Committed
Belonging/ Esteem	Good at it	Direct	Understanding	Contributing
Physiological/ Safety	Good for me	Indirect	Awareness	Compliant

---

[2] Abraham H. Maslow, 1943. "A Theory of Human Motivation," *Psychological Review* 50 (4): 370–96.

Communication Engagement Levels

Communication to Produce for Each Level

Compliance: Those who will comply are concerned about their physiological and safety needs. They focus on things that are good for them. All they need is indirect communication to make them aware of what they need to do so they can comply.

Contribution: Those ready to contribute have graduated to focusing on belonging and esteem needs. They're interested in doing more of what they are good at. Communicate with them directly to give them a chance to ask questions so they can understand your intent and thus contribute.

Commitment: At the top of the pyramid are those looking for self-actualization. They are ready to focus on things that are good for others. You must communicate with them on an emotional level to get them to believe in the cause.

Become the Narrator-in-Chief

Allen Schoer, the founder and chairman of the TAI Group, a leadership consultancy, has an interesting take on the power of stories. He suggests that stories yield narrative. Narrative yields meaning. Meaning yields alignment. Alignment yields performance.[3] So, stories matter.

With the right stories, you can influence but not control those committed to the cause. But, you are not going to be the only one telling the stories that communicate the message. Others are going to tell their own stories in their own ways. So you're not the only storyteller, but you can be the narrator-in-chief, guiding others to choose stories that are in line with the core message.

Touch Points

Touch points are points at which those target audiences are *touched* or reached by your message. Effective communication must include multiple touch points in multiple venues. You'll need to determine both the number of people you reach and the frequency with which you touch

---

[3] 2013, presentation to the Executive Forum, November 9.

them. For the key individuals and groups that you want to touch, map out a series of media methods to do so, including face-to-face conversations, phone calls, videoconferences, notes, e-mails, and more general mass and social media communications.

Monitor and Adjust

You are going to lose control of the communication as soon as you start. As people relate what they've heard to others, they will apply their own filters and biases. Shame on you if you're not ready for that. Have a system in place to monitor how your message is being translated. Be ready to capitalize on opportunities and head off issues. Although you can't prepare for every eventuality, if you can think through a range of possible scenarios, you're more likely to be able to use those contingency plans as a starting point for your response.* Determine how you will measure the success of the message. Just getting it out to the audience does not mean that you've been successful. Also, know how often you will measure whether your message is being received as intended.

Know Your Message. Live Your Message

Peter was brought in to head the telemarketing group for an insurance products company. He had done his due diligence and recognized that the company faced some serious issues. The company had a higher cost structure, but historically had a better closing ratio because of a heavy emphasis on face-to-face selling.

To fend off the increased competition and declining market share, the previous head of telemarketing had implemented several much-needed changes, with the biggest one being a new phone software system. Before launching the new technology, Peter's predecessor failed to get buy-in from key stakeholders regarding the reasons behind the changes. As a result, the technology rollout was a disaster and pitted the telemarketers and field reps against each other. Tempers were high and both groups were blaming each other for the plummeting leads, sales profitability, and customer satisfaction results.

---

* Shannon Stucky of FTI Consulting explained the importance of this to George. As she and her colleagues in FTI's Special Situations group work across the whole range of stakeholders, they've learned the importance of preparing in advance for the surprises that will have the most impact.

Peter realized that he had to have a coherent message on Day One that would quickly rally his team around a shared purpose. His message on Day One was: "As a unified team we will immediately focus on leveraging our new technology to increase high-quality leads and assure an excellent hand-off with superior responsiveness between the teams to increase sales, profitability, and customer satisfaction."

He then deployed a multipoint communication plan that included one-on-one meetings with key stakeholders, interteam calls, company-wide e-mails, and a new leaders' group to report progress. As the two teams worked together to roll out the many features of the new technology, Peter continuously communicated the reason behind the changes, their benefits, and how they would impact the stated goal.

Peter's Day One message was a valuable stepping-stone to achieve two benchmarks: a historic rate of high-quality leads and closed deals in a record time frame. Along the way, he created a public scorecard for results and constantly communicated the teams' quick progress to all the key stakeholders. To keep the momentum and energy up, he encouraged chatter about the results and further ways to improve.

In very short order, the two teams were rallied around a clear and common goal. Peter's inspiring message was the spark that turned two demoralized groups pointing fingers at each other into one fiery team with the will to win. They reached both benchmarks 30 days early.

Repeat the Message

In your communication efforts, repetition is essential. We'll say it again; repetition is essential. In other words, you're going to have to create different ways and times to repeat the same message over and over again. You'll get bored of your own message well before the critical mass has internalized it, but don't shy away from repeating it. Do not ever let your boredom show; make sure you keep your energy and excitement levels high regarding the message. When you're done, do it again, fitting it into the right context for each audience each time.

Celebrate Early Wins

Somewhere along the way, you will have identified an early win for your first six months. As part of this campaign, you will have overinvested to deliver that win. When it is complete, celebrate it, and celebrate it publicly. This is all about giving the team confidence in itself. So invest your time to make the team members feel great.

Reinforce

There is going to be a crisis of confidence at some point. At that point the team will question whether you're really serious about these changes and whether the changes you are making are going to stick. Be ready for the crisis and use that moment to reinforce your efforts.

The first thing you need is an early warning system to see the crisis developing. By this time you should be able to tap other eyes and ears throughout the organization to get an on-the-street read of the situation. These are going to be people who feel safe telling you what's really going on. They might be administrative staff, those outside your direct line of reports, or people far enough removed from you that they don't feel threatened telling you the truth. Whoever they are, you need to identify them and cultivate them.

The main sign of the impending crisis will be the naysayers or detractors raising their heads and their objections again or more boldly. It is likely they will go quiet during the period of initial enthusiasm after the launch of the Burning Imperative. But they will usually find it impossible to stay quiet forever. Their return to nay saying will be the first signs of the crisis, and their point of view will spread if you don't cut it off.

So hit the restart button fast. Make it clear that you are committed to the changes. Regroup your core team to confirm its commitment. Positively recognize supporters, those making an effort to drive the team change imperative. And, take action against the blocking coalitions, with negative consequences ranging from feedback to moving people off the team if they are hindrances to business and cultural progress. Some good steps at this point may include:

- Regroup with your core team to gather input and adjust as appropriate
- *All-hands* meetings, videoconferences, or calls to highlight progress and reinforce the Burning Imperative
- Follow-up note confirming the commitment to the Burning Imperative

- Follow-up phone calls with each individual on the core team
- Reinforce Burning Imperative at each key milestone with core team, their teams, and others
- Meetings or one-on-ones with key people or groups at a level below your direct reports
- Field or plant visits
- Implement a structured monitoring plan
- Introduce a reward and recognition program to reinforce strong performance and supporting behaviors

HOT TIP

Think in terms of a network of communication: Discover your core message. Then use that to guide key communication points in an iterative set of concurrent conversations across a network of multiple stakeholders and a wide variety of media, all built on a foundation of trustworthy authenticity. Effective communication is hard work. But it will be one of the most important and most enduring things you do.

At Charley Shimanski's first conference as head of the American Red Cross disaster response operations, he hosted 140 disaster response directors and other colleagues.

It was a master class in communication. Charley was everywhere: on the stage introducing speakers, speaking himself, reconnecting with old friends, hugging people who had gone through tough response engagements. He owned the room and reinforced the attendees' passion for the cause. His message flowed from every action, every message, and every pore of his being.

When asked about how he prepared for a session like that, Charley explained that he doesn't think about what he's going to say and he doesn't think about what he wants his audience to hear. Instead, he thinks about how he wants them to feel.

"I wanted them to feel that they are at the core of what we do, that our success is on their shoulders. I wanted them to feel proud."

On the one hand, not everyone has a cause as generally meaningful as the Red Cross disaster response mission: *"Provide relief to victims of disasters and help people prevent, prepare for, and respond to emergencies."*

But you have a cause that is meaningful to you and to the people you're leading. If it didn't matter, you wouldn't be there. Be. Do. Say. Communicate the message in what you say. Communicate it in what you do. Make it your own. Do that and those following you will commit to it. You'll all feel proud.

Activate Ongoing Communication: Summary and Implications

- **Phasing matters.** Between Day One and setting the Burning Imperative, go slowly. You're still converging, still listening and learning.

- **Stakeholders.** Take into account the network of multiple stakeholders as you specifically identify your target audiences. Relook at your up, down, and across stakeholders and contributors, detractors, and watchers to gauge their level of engagement.

- **Message.** Gear your communication approach differently to those with different levels of engagement. Relook at and leverage your overarching message as the foundation for guiding iterative, concurrent conversations by seeding and reinforcing communication points through a wide variety of media with no compromises on trustworthiness and authenticity. At the most senior leadership levels, you should think about yourself as the narrator-in-chief, setting the direction for others' stories.

- **Flex.** Modify for your various audiences while maintaining your core message.

- **Adjust.** Monitor and adjust as appropriate on an ongoing basis.

- **Old School.** Don't hesitate to deploy an old-school logical, sequential communication campaign when appropriate—though expect that to be the case less and less over time.

QUESTIONS YOU SHOULD ASK YOURSELF

Am I modifying my messages for different audiences?

Am I clear what behaviors I want from my audience(s)?

Is the content of my message compelling?

Have I considered the optimal design (form, venue) for each specific communication?

Have I designed a means of evaluating the effectiveness of my communications?

Does my communication approach reach all the key stakeholders in the best way for each of them?

Additional Articles and Tools on www.onboardingtools.com

4A.1   Press Interviews

4A.2   15 Secrets to Becoming a Great Communicator

TOOL 4.1
Communication Guide[†]

Use this tool to plan out your ongoing communication.

Target Audience

Core target

Primary influencers

Other influencers

**Desired Behaviors
(e.g., understanding,
alignment, commitment,
action)**

Core Message

Communication Points

Promise

Reason to believe

Supporting examples

Media

Off-line/live

Online

Social

Tracking

How to measure success?

How often to measure?

Contingency plans?

CHAPTER 5

Pivot to Strategy

CO-CREATE THE BURNING IMPERATIVE BY DAY 30.

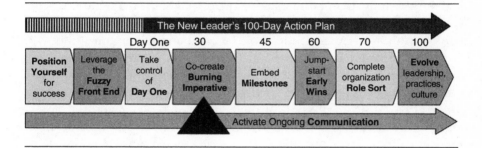

You can control your schedule during the Fuzzy Front End—mostly because no one expects you to do anything. You probably can control your schedule on Day One or, at least, have a big influence on it—mostly because no one expects you to have thought it through as much as you will have after reading this book. You will have far less control over the rest of your first 100 days—because all sorts of people will be putting all sorts of demands on your time. Carving out team-building time is going to be tough. But building a high-performing team is essential. So make the time.

Creating the Burning Imperative

On top of everything else you have to do, and all the other demands on your schedule, make the time to implement the building blocks of tactical capacity. The starting point, and indeed the foundation, is the Burning Imperative with its components of headline, mission, vision, values, objectives, goals, strategies, plans, and operating cadence. Experienced, successful leaders inevitably say that getting people aligned around a vision and values and focused on urgent business matters are the most important things they have to do—and often the most difficult during their first 100 days.

The Burning Imperative is a clear, sharply defined, intensely shared, and purposefully urgent understanding from all of the team members of what they are "supposed to do, now" and how this Burning Imperative works with the larger aspirations of the team and the organization.

The Burning Imperative must have a shorthand summary or headline—most likely containing a strong, action-oriented verb. This is a brief statement, or tagline, that reminds team members of the entire range of work—from mission through strategy to plans, and the statements behind each step—and specifically of their commitments and responsibilities in relation to that work. For example, "Establish a Burning Imperative by Day 30."

A Burning Imperative is different from a shared purpose. The difference between the two is timing, intensity, and duration. The shared purpose drives the long term while your Burning Imperative drives the next phase of activity, now, on the way to the long term.

Remember the Apollo 13 example of "Get these men home alive." Clear. Sharply defined. Intensely shared. Purposefully urgent. It trumps all petty concerns. It didn't replace the overall shared purpose of exploring the universe to increase man's knowledge. The Burning Imperative moves the team forward to that longer-term shared purpose. That's what you're aiming for.

We all saw the same thing in northern Chile in 2010 when 33 miners were trapped for 69 days 2,230 feet below the ground. Almost no one thought that the rescuers would ever retrieve the bodies, let alone pull them out alive. But after 17 days of being trapped underground without contact with anyone, the miners sent a message to the surface that they were all alive! Instantly, the Burning Imperative was set: "Get these men out alive!" No one had a plan on how to get it done when the Burning Imperative was set, but the rescue team, with help from people around the world, invented a way to get those men home safely. That is a Burning Imperative at work!

Don't Hesitate to Burn Rubber on the Way to a Burning Imperative

The Burning Imperative drives the primary focus of the leadership team every day. More than any single other factor, this is what distinguishes highly successful teams from teams that flounder and fail. More than any other single factor, this is the key to surviving and thriving in and accelerating a complex transition. This is the heart of tactical capacity. Teams with a clear Burning Imperative can be more flexible in their actions and reactions because each individual team member can be confident that his or her team members are heading in the same direction.

Not everyone agrees on how fast you should move to get this in place. The argument for stretching out this process is that the risks of picking the wrong Burning Imperative are greater than the risks of moving too slowly. There have certainly been cases where this has been true. If things are going well, there's less urgency to change things.

However, failing to build momentum early can create problems of its own. If some negative external factor intervenes before you have started to move forward (e.g., you lose a key customer or a vital team member leaves), you may fall into a debacle. We all have seen that the pace of change is accelerating as information flows more and more freely. In that environment, even if things are going well, competitors are going to converge rapidly on your position.

You need to move quickly. Today, it is better to get moving and adapt as appropriate. How fast should you move on this? Fast. Get this in place by the end of your first 30 days.

Harold was 100 days into his new role as vice president of marketing for a $1 billion manufacturing company when his boss asked him to pick up business development as well. (Harold had handled the initial steps of his complex transition well indeed.) So Harold hit a restart button with the new team, pulling them together for a Burning Imperative workshop.

The company had experienced serious problems from an unbalanced pipeline in the past but had been unable to frame the problem and the solution. The team members agreed that their Burning Imperative had to be one that drove them to "create opportunities beyond the current horizon."

After robust discussion, they determined that to achieve their goals they needed 10 new high-level prospect meetings, 10 new contracts, and 10 final deliverables accomplished within the year. The team created a tagline for the Burning Imperative: 10-10-10! They also gained agreement on the underlying mission statement, vision, values, objectives, and goals as well as the strategies, plans, and operating cadence that flowed from those. Everybody walked away from the workshop with an absolutely clear and precise sense of the role the team was to play in driving the Burning Imperative. The rallying cry was "10-10-10!" and everyone was energized by his or her personal call to action in support of that.

What emerged from this Burning Imperative was clear alignment across all three main parties—business development, senior management, and delivery team. Each group had to work across all parts of the pipeline, with delivery helping business development with new prospect meetings, business development helping the delivery team lock down actual delivery (managing expectations and timetable), and senior management paying close attention to the balance and rhythm of resources and pitching in directly as needed.

What was extraordinary was not so much what they did, but how fast they got it done. From the moment this team first came together until the time the chief executive officer (CEO) approved the plans, only 30 hours had elapsed. To achieve this, the team followed the outline as detailed in the Burning Imperative workshop (Tool 5.1) at the end of this chapter. On its completion, one member of the team said, "I've been here six years. It's the first time I've known what I was supposed to do."

HOT TIP

The Burning Imperative: This is the centerpiece of tactical capacity. When people talk about getting everyone on the same page, this is that page. Use whatever methodology you would like to get it in place. But do be sure to get it in place and get buy-in early. In a hot landing when there is an acute need for the team members to act, it's imperative that they do so quickly. It is not that there are just diminishing returns to doing this after Day 30; there is an actual cliff. After Day 30, the sense of urgency dissipates almost immediately and things start slipping precariously. So you really need to do whatever it takes to get this done by Day 30. This is a big deal.

Burning Imperative Components

The components of the Burning Imperative are headline, mission, vision, values, objectives, goals, strategies, plans, and operating cadence. Together, these drive the team's actual plans and actions.

Headline: The all-encapsulating phrase or tagline that defines your Burning Imperative.

Mission: *Why* here, why exist, what business are we in?

Vision: Future picture—*what* we want to become, where we are going.

Values: Beliefs and moral principles that guide and underpin attitudes, relationships, and behaviors.

Objectives: Broadly defined, qualitative performance requirements.

Goals: The quantitative measures of the objectives that define success.

Strategies: Broad choices around *how* the team will achieve its objectives.

Plans: The most important projects and initiatives that will bring each strategy to fruition.

Operating Cadence: How the team is going to implement, track, and evolve plans, together.

People often confuse the difference between a mission and a vision. Sometimes people just combine the two. But they are different. A mission guides what people do every day and why it matters. It informs what roles need to exist in the organization. A vision is the picture of *what* future success will look like. It helps define areas where the organization needs to be best in class* and helps keep everyone aware of the essence of the company.

Similarly, people confuse objectives and goals. Objectives connect qualitatively with the vision. (Example: Move past competitor A to become the preferred provider in the market.) Goals must be quantita-

---

* *Best in class* means better than anyone else—superiority. *World-class* means in a class with the best—parity. Both are dramatically different from *good enough*.

tive. They must be specific, measurable, achievable, realistic, and time bound (SMART). (Example: Increase revenue by 10 percent in each product category in each of the next three years.)

Teams will often resort to a tagline referring to a goal (such as "10-10-10!"). But as the leader, you need to make sure you keep connecting this with the objective. (Ensure a stable pipeline of new business and deliver reliably against it!) Sometimes the mission works as a headline. Sometimes the vision or priorities work. It doesn't matter. All that matters is getting everyone on the same page.

Make It Happen

How do you build the individual elements—mission, vision, values, and so on—and roll them up into a Burning Imperative? You and your core team need to invest time and work into conceiving, shaping, articulating, and communicating each element and then helping translate these into a unified Burning Imperative that works as a headline for the entire plan and that focuses individuals on their particular roles and responsibilities. It may seem daunting, but once it gets going and the team connects with the project, it develops a momentum and urgency of its own. The light clicking on for the team is one of the most exciting and memorable feelings that you and your team will ever have.

There are different ways to do this. If you don't have confidence in your team, a consultative approach tends to work best. In this case, you would draft a first-cut Burning Imperative and then get everyone else's input one at a time. This way you never lose control of the conversation.

The workshop tool in this chapter (Tool 5.1) is designed to help you and your team reach consensus on your mission, vision, values, objectives, goals, strategies, plans, and operating cadence.

The operative word is *co-creation*. You probably already have some of the components (mission, vision, objectives, strategies, etc.) in your head. They may even be down on paper. Your team members may have told you that they agree. But, do they know them off the top of their heads? Do they (did they ever) really believe them? Are the components current? Inspiring? Do they create a sense of urgency and drive purposeful action? Do team members really see what they're doing as a

Burning Imperative or just as something nice to do to pass the time? Your job as a leader is to make sure that everyone on the team can genuinely answer yes to those questions.

Bryan Smith lays out different ways of rolling out ideas: telling, selling, testing, consulting, and co-creating.[1] In most cases the best approach is co-creating. The rewards of creating together are so immense and so memorable that the process alone is the strongest antidote to silos, confusion, and indifference. You don't want the team members thinking that their mission is just a slew of buzzwords that you threw at them. Sadly, that is the destiny of many so-called Burning Imperatives.

The premise behind the Burning Imperative workshop is to co-create the Burning Imperative with your core team so that all share it. After the meeting, you should test the Burning Imperative by letting others in the organization consult with your core team. They may have perspectives that will lead to slight tweaks. You should be open to wording changes and some new ideas during the test, but be careful to preserve the meaning of the Burning Imperative that you and your team co-created.

Do not make the mistake of attempting to let your entire organization co-create your Burning Imperative. In general, the ideal meeting size is between five to nine people. Groups of fewer than five people struggle to find enough diversity in their thinking. Groups of more than nine struggle for airtime. Additionally, if the co-creating team is too large, you're likely to end up with something that is acceptable to most and inspirational to none. By co-creating with just your core team, and perhaps one or two other key players, you can lead the team toward more inspirational ideas.

Done right, a Burning Imperative workshop is an intensive session with a lot of personal sharing and dialogue. Expect to learn a lot about your team members and colleagues. Expect them to learn a lot about you. It is possible that you'll end up with a Burning Imperative very close to what you came in with. It is more likely

---

[1] Peter M. Senge, Art Kleiner, Charlotte Roberts, Richard B. Ross, Bryan J. Smith, 1994, *The Fifth Discipline Fieldbook* (Boston: Nicholas Brealey).

that you won't. Even if you do, there's power for all in the learning. As T. S. Eliot says in "Little Gidding":

We shall not cease from exploration.
And the end of all our exploring
Will be to arrive where we started
And know the place for the first time.[2]

Workshop Attendance and Timing

In the real world, you'll be taking over an existing team with existing priorities and existing schedules. It is unlikely that your team members will have planned to take out two days from their current work to sit around, hold hands, and sing folk songs. First point, this is real work, and the Burning Imperative workshop tool is focused on real business issues. It ends up being a strong team-building exercise, but as a by-product of the work. Even so, there will be some team members who are reluctant to adjust their existing schedules to accommodate this workshop, particularly if you push to hold it sometime in your first 30 days.

Stick with the plan. Find the date in your first 30 days that works best for most people, and then give the others the option to change their schedules or not. This approach has two advantages:

1. It keeps things moving forward in line with the 80 percent rule. Not everything is going to be perfect. Not everyone can be at every meeting. You and your team will move forward as best as you can, helping others catch up and adjusting along the way.

2. It gives you early data about different team members' attitudes and commitment. Everything communicates, and everything communicates both ways. By inviting people to a Burning Imperative workshop, you are sending a powerful message. Their turning it down because they have something more important to do returns a different message. How you handle overt resistance will be an important early test of your assimilate, converge and evolve, or shock (ACES) model (Chapter 2).

---

[2] 1943, in *Four Quartets* (New York: Harcourt Brace).

HOT TIP

In most cases, to establish an environment of co-creation, it is best if you, as the leader, do not facilitate the Burning Imperative workshop. Being a participant as opposed to the facilitator puts you in a better position to listen and understand your team's input and perspective, which will help you craft a truly co-created Burning Imperative. The dynamics alone of you sitting with the team as opposed to leading in front of the room tends to foster a richer and more honest dialogue from the team. It's not about you. You want to emerge with a *team's* Burning Imperative, not the *leader's*.

Follow through Consistently

Follow through and then follow through again. Pulling people together, investing the time in this, and then not living by it is worse than not doing it at all. A strong Burning Imperative is a covenant of honor. Once you put it in place, you must live it if you expect people to follow your lead. You must follow through on your commitments. You must support people who flex standard procedures in pursuit of the Burning Imperative.

Gerry was a volunteer with his local life squad/ambulance service. One day he heard an accident while raking leaves in his front lawn. He ran down to the end of the street and started treating the victims, enrolling bystanders to summon the police, life squad, and help in other ways. Two of the victims walked away and two had to be taken to the hospital.

After the run to the hospital, Gerry was at the station helping to clean out the ambulance for the next call when the life squad captain walked in.

"Gerry, I noticed you were on the scene of this accident without your red life squad coat on."

Gerry explained why he had gone straight to the scene without putting his coat on, going to the station, and riding with the ambulance even though he had been on call.

"But wearing your coat is important so people can identify you as a life squad member."

"Good point. I'll be careful the next time. . . . Wait a minute. How did you notice I wasn't wearing my coat?"

"I drove by."

"Are you telling me you drove by the scene of a two-car accident, saw that I was the only life squad member there, and you chose to come by here and remind me to wear my coat the next time? How about stopping to help!"

It doesn't matter what words they actually used. The underlying Burning Imperative of every life squad, ambulance team, or first responder of any sort must be "Help people in need." This life squad captain was not living the message. You must.

If you are unclear about the differences between all these things and how they work together, stop. Go to www.onboardingtools.com for a more detailed explanation. It will be well worth your time to get familiar with these basic building blocks.

Focus

Let's talk about the power of focus. The best way to lead your team to the desired results is to drive a message you are passionate about with as few points as possible and ideally one main, overriding imperative. So what's your team's focus? It's a lesson masterly reinforced by Steve Jobs and J.K. Rowling.

Jobs

In his 2005 commencement speech at Stanford, Steve Jobs told three stories to make three points:

1. Follow your heart.
2. Don't settle.
3. Don't live someone else's life.

In one way, or another, all three points communicate the same thing: Figure out what really matters and why. Put all your energy into overcoming the obstacles you can, accepting the things you must, and connecting with those that matter. Focus.

As chronicled in the many books about his life, Jobs' passionate focus on what he thought was ultimately important changed the world for the better—in ways that most of us have felt.

Rowling

In her 2008 commencement speech at Harvard, J.K. Rowling focused on two points:

1. The value of failure
2. The power of imagination

Rowling first came up with the idea of the Harry Potter series when she was stuck on a train in 1990. At the time, she lived in relative poverty and was about to enter one of the darkest periods of her life, which included a divorce and the loss of her mother. Yet she kept her focus and seven years later introduced Harry Potter to the world. Six sequels followed.

Focus is what allowed her to move from poverty in 1990 to establishing her own charity, the Volant Charitable Trust, in 2000 (with a multimillion-dollar annual budget) to fight poverty and social inequality. Both she and Jobs imagined new worlds. Both had extraordinary focus. Both made a huge impact.

There is real power in focusing as much of your energy as you can on the one thing you care most about. Figure out what's important. Manage the distractions and focus.

- Focusing on one Burning Imperative rallies the team.
- Delivering one early win gives the team confidence.
- Driving one overriding message improves communication and buy-in.

Pivot to Strategy: Summary and Implications

The Burning Imperative consists of:

Headline: The all-encapsulating phrase or tagline that defines your Burning Imperative.

Mission: *Why* here, why exist, what business are you in?

Vision: Future picture—*what* you want to become; where are you going?

Values: Beliefs and moral principles that guide and underpin attitudes, relationships, and behaviors.

Objectives: Broadly defined, qualitative performance requirements.

Goals: The quantitative measures of the objectives that define success.

Strategies: Broad choices around *how* the team will achieve its objectives.

Plans: The most important projects and initiatives that will bring each strategy to fruition.

Operating Cadence: How the team is going to implement, track, and evolve plans, together.

The Burning Imperative is the pivot point for the new leader's first 100 days. Once this is established, the team moves into creating and leveraging the next wave of tactical capacity building blocks—milestone management, early wins, role sort, and evolution of leadership, practices, and culture.

For the Burning Imperative to drive everything everyone actually does every day, it must be truly embraced by all. Thus, you need to get it in place and shared early on—within your first 30 days at the latest. A two- to three-day facilitated workshop is the preferred model for making that happen.

QUESTIONS YOU SHOULD ASK YOURSELF

Have we laid the right foundation on which to build a high-performing team?

Have we done the prework with the team to have a successful workshop?

Have we co-created a Burning Imperative?

Is it compelling enough to the key stakeholders?

Can the team clearly identify our focus?

Do we have the strategies and defined goals to make it real?

Does it drive purposeful action?

Is it aligned to and is it a step toward achieving our long-term purpose?

Additional Articles and Tools on
www.onboardingtools.com

5A.1   Strategic Planning
5A.2   Business Plan Elements
5A.3   Profit Pools
5A.4   Financial Forecasts
5A.5   Mission, Vision, Values Discussion Guides
5A.6   Where Play Choices

Burning Imperative Workshop[†]

This is a two- to three-day, off-site workshop to drive consensus around mission, vision, values, objectives, goals, strategies, plans, and operating cadence. All members of the core team must attend. This workshop will determine the team's Burning Imperative.

Preparation

- In premeeting communications, set a clear destination for the meeting (mission, vision, values, objectives, goals, strategies, plans, operating cadence).

- Set context—current reality—broader group's purpose.

- Send invitations, set logistics.

- Prepare to present your current best thinking (leader), or prepare to explain your role (team members).

Delivery

- Detail the destination: framework, mission, vision, values, objectives, goals, strategies, plans, operating cadence (facilitator).

- Present the current best thinking (team leader).

- Present the current subgroup roles (team members).

- Set up what matters and why.

- Review the corporate/larger group purpose (team leader).

TOOL 5.1   Burning Imperative Workshop (continued)

- Revise the team's mission, vision, values, objectives, goals, strategies, plans, and operating cadence in turn by encouraging an open but focused discussion to expand ideas, group them into similar categories, select the ones that resonate most, rank them in order of importance, solicit individual drafts, collect common thoughts, and create a group draft based on input that includes the Burning Imperative headline (facilitator).
- Discuss how the new Burning Imperative is different from the old situation (facilitator).
- Summarize what it will take to achieve the Burning Imperative (facilitator).
- Wrap up, tie the results back to the destination, and communicate the next steps (including establishing dates for defining milestone management and early wins processes).

Follow-Up

- Share with broader team for its input.
- Make refinements if required.
- Communicate the final results to all key stakeholders.

Drive Operational Accountability

EMBED MILESTONES BY DAY 45 AND EARLY WINS BY DAY 60.

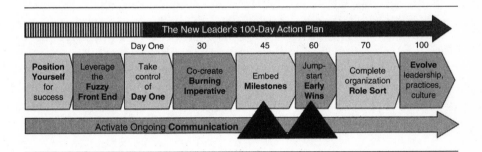

The New Leader's 100-Day Action Plan

he real test of a high-performing team's tactical capacity lies in the formal and informal practices that are at work across team members, particularly around clarifying decision rights and information flows.[1] The real job of a high-performing team's leader is to inspire and enable others to do their absolute best, together. These leaders spend more time integrating across than managing down. This is best achieved by implementing a straightforward milestone management tool that focuses on mapping and tracking who is doing what, by when. High-performing team leaders exploit this milestone management tool to hold each other accountable and enable people to work together as a team!

---

[1] Gary L. Neilson, Karla L. Martin, and Elizabeth Powers, 2008, "The Secrets to Successful Strategy Execution," *Harvard Business Review*, June.

Early wins are all about credibility and confidence. People have more faith in people who have delivered. You want team members to have confidence in you, in themselves, and in the plan for change that has emerged. You want your boss to have confidence in you. Early wins fuel that confidence. To that end, identify and jump-start potential early wins by Day 60, and overinvest to deliver them by the end of your first six months—as a team!

Capture the Milestones

Milestones are the building blocks of tactical capacity that turn a Burning Imperative into a manageable action plan. Your team's milestone management practice, if done right, will be a powerful team reinforcer. This is all about follow-through. Burning Imperative meetings tend to produce many ideas and choices on flip charts. They are all completely useless unless someone takes action to make them happen. This chapter is about ensuring that they do. In brief, to help ensure that the team delivers the desired results, in the time frame specified, you should strive for absolute clarity around:

- Decision rights—who can decide what, who is the ultimate decision maker
- Accountabilities—who owes delivery of specific items
- Linkages—what interdependencies exist with other teams and projects
- Information flows—what information needs to be shared with and by whom
- Collaboration—what joint efforts are needed to ensure alignment and adherence

Rarely is the delivery of a milestone reliant on one person. More often than not a milestone requires contributions from several members of the team across many functions. Despite the complexity of delivery, each milestone should be assigned one "captain" who is ultimately accountable for the delivery of that milestone. The captain is not the person required to do all the work, but rather the key spokesperson for the communication of issues regarding that milestone. The captain should be the final decision maker, responsible for communicating across groups, ensuring needed information flows, collaboration, and delivery of the final result. Avoid cocaptains. They never work. There needs to be a single point of accountability.

Follow through—Or Don't Even Start

Sam's team put a lot of time and energy into creating a Burning Imperative during a two-day workshop. The team left excited and ready to move forward. Then Sam got busy and never put the milestone management process in place. As a result, the team quickly went back to doing things the way it had been doing them before. If Sam wasn't going to follow through, why should the team?

Practices are the systems that enable people to implement the plans. They need to be coupled with systems of metrics and rewards that reinforce the desired behaviors. There is an old saying: "Show me how they are paid and I'll tell you what they really do."

John Michael Loh, U.S. Air Force Air Combat Command, during the first Gulf War said: "I used to believe that if it doesn't get measured, it doesn't get done. Now I say if it doesn't get measured it doesn't get approved. . . . You need to manage by facts, not gut feel." As Michael Bloomberg, the former mayor of New York City put it, "You're entitled to your own opinions, but not your own facts."[2]

Specific performance measurements, accountabilities, and decision rights free people and teams to do their jobs without undue interference and provide the basis for nonjudgmental discussion of performance versus expectations and how to make improvements. It is essential that people know what is expected of them. When the expectations are clear, people also must have the time and resources needed to deliver against those expectations. The milestone management process is focused on clarifying decision rights and making sure that information and resources flow to where they need to go.

Milestones Are Checkpoints along the Way to a Defined Goal

Recall these definitions from Chapter 5:

> **Objectives:** Broadly defined, qualitative performance requirements.

---

[2] 2008, commencement address, University of Pennsylvania, Philadelphia, May.

Goals: The quantitative measures of the objectives that define success.

Strategies: Broad choices around how the team will achieve its objectives.

Now add:

Milestones: Checkpoints along the way to achieving objectives and goals.

The National Aeronautics and Space Administration (NASA) and the Apollo 13 ground team provide a useful example of this. The objective of getting the astronauts back home alive after the explosion in space was compelling, but overwhelming.

It was easier to work through milestones one by one:

1. Turn the ship around so it would get back to Earth.
2. Manage the remaining power so it would last until the astronauts were back.
3. Fix the carbon monoxide problem so the air remained breathable.
4. Manage reentry into the atmosphere so the ship didn't burn up.

The power of milestones is that they let you know how you're doing along the way and give you the opportunity to make adjustments. They also give you the comfort to let your team run toward the goal without your involvement, as long as the milestones are being reached as planned.

You might evaluate your team's journey to a goal like this:

Worst case: The team misses a goal and doesn't know why.

Bad: The team misses a goal and does know why.

Okay: The team misses a milestone but adjusts to make the overall goal.

Hit: The team anticipates a risk and adjusts along the way to hit key milestones.

Best: The team hits all its milestones on the way to delivering its goals. (In your dreams.)

Imagine that you set a goal of getting from London to Paris in 5½ hours. Now imagine that you choose to drive. Imagine further that it takes you 45 minutes to get from central London to the outskirts of London. You wonder: "How's the trip going so far?"

You have no clue.

You might be on track. You might be behind schedule. But it's early in the trip, so you probably think that you can make up time later if you need to. So you're not worried.

If, on the other hand, you had set the following milestones, you would be thinking differently:

- Central London to outskirts of London: 30 minutes.
- Outskirts of London to Folkestone: 70 minutes.
- Channel crossing: load: 20 minutes; cross: 20 minutes; unload: 20 minutes.
- Calais to Paris: 3 hours.

If you had set a milestone of getting to the outskirts of London in 30 minutes and it took you 45 minutes, you would know you were behind schedule. Knowing that you were behind schedule, you could then take action on alternative options. The milestone would make you immediately aware of the need to adjust to still reach your overall goal.

You and your team are going to miss milestones. It is not necessary to hit all your milestones. What is essential is that you have put in place a mechanism to identify reasonable milestones so that you have checkpoints that allow you to anticipate and adjust along the way to hitting your final destination on time.

Manage Milestone Updates with a Five-Step Process

Deploying a mutually supportive, team-based follow-up system helps everyone improve performance related to goals. Organizations that have deployed this process in their team meetings have seen dramatic improvements in team performance. Follow these steps as well as the prep and post instructions laid out here and in Tool 6.1, and you'll be well on your way to ensuring that the team achieves its desired results on time.

Step 1. Prep. Circulate individual milestone updates to the team to read before each meeting so you can take update sharing and reporting off the agenda, while deploying a disciplined process to make sure that information flows where it needs to go.

Executives often skip this step, much to the team's detriment. It seems like an easy process to put in place, but we've heard every reason in the book as to why it has not been implemented.

Usually there are some logistical protocols that need to be established, tracking method choices and time frames established for submitting and distribution of information before the process can begin. You must require that everyone complete the update and premeeting review on time. If you allow excuses here, the rest of the process takes a hit. Yes, it can be a pain to get it started, but once it is embedded as a team expectation and value, you'll be thankful that you endured the brief period of pain. Just do it. Trust us.

Step 2. Report. Use the first half of each meeting for each team member to headline wins, learnings, and areas in which the person needs help from other team members. Resist the typical urge to work through items at this point.

Discussing items here—as opposed to simply reporting status—reinforces a first-come, first-served mentality where the people who share later in the order tend to get squeezed for time. This is an inefficient use of time. Removing the discussion piece from the first half of the meeting opens up time to identify "where I need help from team members." This is often the most important part of the meeting. Each of these items should be captured in real time. It's a good idea to keep a set time limit for each individual update. Those who tend to be long-winded might not like it, but the rest of the participants will appreciate it. A tight and controlled limit goes a long way toward making the meetings more dynamic.

Step 3. Prioritize. Pause at the meeting's halfway point to prioritize items for discussion so the team can discuss items in the right priority instead of first-come, first-served.

These won't necessarily be the universally most important items because some items should be worked on with a different group or subset of the team. You should make note of those items in the meeting, but defer them to another meeting where the full and proper group can address them. Instead, give priority to the most important items *for this team* to work on *as a team, at this time*. Tend to give priority to items that are off target, in danger, or in areas where help is needed. Develop a list in descending order of priority.

Step 4. Problem solve. Use the second part of the meeting to discuss, in order, the priority list you determined to be the overall team's most important issues and opportunities.

The expectation is that the team won't get through all the items. That's okay because you're working on the most important items first. (Which is why you paused to prioritize.) This is the time to figure out how to adjust as a team to achieve the most important goals, all the while reinforcing predetermined decision rights.

We suggest an approach to group problem solving that is particularly appropriate for these conversations (see Tool 6.3):

1. Share pre-reading to let people think about the problem and potential solutions in advance. This pre-reading should include, at a minimum: the problem, current best thinking, context, and some potential options.

2. Start with the problem owner's current best thinking. (You'll need clarity around who is the problem owner and who is the decision maker.)

3. Decide whether the group will discuss the problem. If yes:

4. Answer questions for clarification (to help people understand context and current best thinking, not for them to comment on or improve the thinking—yet).

5. Highlight the most positive aspects of the current best thinking contributing to making it work.

6. Identify barriers keeping the current best thinking from working. (Get all the barriers on the table at the same time before working on any of them.)

7. Decide on the most important barrier.

8. Direct a brainstorm on the most important barrier with all participating, including the problem owner. Look for statements from the team members that might help remedy the barrier. Require statements to be in the *What you do is* . . . (WYDIS) format.

9. The problem owner considers and pulls together a possible remedy to that barrier. Test it with the group.

10. If the tested remedy is not strong enough, continue to work on this barrier. If the remedy works, determine whether that is enough to solve the overall problem. If yes, move on to action steps. If not, work on the next most important barrier.

11. Action steps: Agree who will do what, by when, now that this problem is solved.

Step 5. Close the loop. Defer other items to the next meeting or to a separate meeting. Update the tracking reports with any changes or new directions. Communicate major shifts to those key stakeholders who need to know.

HOT TIP 1

It's best if people have had the opportunity to think about the problem and potential solutions in advance, before the meeting. Encourage people to share relevant documents, analysis, and questions before the meeting. This prereading should include, at a minimum, the problem, the current best thinking, the context, and some potential options.

HOT TIP 2

Anticipation is the key: At first, milestones will go from "on track" to "oops we missed" with no steps in between. You'll know the process is working when people are surfacing areas they "might miss" if they don't get help from others. Focus your love and attention on these "might miss" items to get the team to help. It will make people feel good about surfacing issues and will encourage them to bring future issues to the group for help.

HOT TIP 3

Banish the first-come, first-served mentality. This milestone process is easy to deploy for disciplined people and teams. It is hard for less disciplined people because they want to work items first-come, first-served. Resist that. Follow the process. You'll learn to love it. (Well, maybe not love it, but you will appreciate it. It will strengthen your team.)

HOT TIP 4

Integrate across instead of managing down. The milestone meetings are great forums for making connections across groups. The higher you rise in the organization, the more time you'll spend integrating across and the less time you'll spend managing down. Senior managers don't like to be managed from above or have their decision rights compromised, but everyone appreciates improved information flows and linkage of projects and priorities across groups.

Use Milestone Management to Lead Postmerger Integration

For Warren, milestone management was the critical tool to drive the myriad of projects needed to integrate an equal-sized acquired business into his private equity–owned business services company.

First, the Burning Imperative workshop identified eight complex strategies that would ensure a successful integration. Warren set the tone for milestone management during that session, making it clear that there would be high expectations for on-time delivery of agreed-upon plans.

During the workshop, Warren appointed captains from both the acquiring and the acquired company to lead each strategy. He gave the captains full authority and told them he expected full cooperation, open information flows, and collaboration across the two organizations. At the end of the Burning Imperative he made it clear that each team member, regardless of where he or she came from, was expected to contribute and lead for the newly combined entity.

Next, during the milestone meetings, Warren communicated the process in advance and followed it with rigor. He challenged longtime members of his team as much as he did new members. The meetings' focus was all about the plans and progress against the milestones.

Almost immediately the milestone management meetings became *the* primary venue for cross-functional, cross-project, and cross-company communication. Not only did the discipline deliver tangible business results, but within several weeks, it was also clear the two teams were united in their shared purpose and commitment to project deliverables.

The practices of communication, joint problem solving, and accountability to each other became a galvanizing force that drove their team success.

Use Milestone Management at the Board Level

Garr's board meetings were out of control. Individual board members kept taking the meetings' agendas offtrack in order to emphasize their own favorite issues.

To combat this, Garr put in place a milestone management process.

Each board member submitted his or her updates to the board secretary ahead of the board meeting. The secretary then compiled them and sent them back to everyone at least 48 hours in advance of the board meetings.

At the 2-hour board meetings, the first hour was spent with the 24 board members giving 2-minute recaps of their updates, emphasizing the areas where they needed help or thought more discussion was warranted.

At the halfway point, the board president looked at all the outstanding issues and ordered them from highest priority to lowest priority.

The board spent the next hour working through the issues in priority order, not worrying about time. They never got through the entire list in the meetings. But that was okay because the issues they got to were more important than the issues that had to be discussed later.

This schedule revolutionized the board meetings. Everyone got 2 minutes in the spotlight. Everyone got a chance to raise issues. But the agenda was no longer managed on a first-come, first-served basis. As a result, the board could spend more time on the more important issues.

Early Wins

There is often a conversation about six months after a leader has started a new role. Someone will ask the new leader's boss how the new leader is doing. You have probably taken part in these conversations before.

"By the way, how's that new leader Rhonda doing?"

"Rhonda? She's fabulous. Love the intelligence. Love the attitude. She may be off to a slow start. But what a great hire! Really like her."

Result: Rhonda's probably on the way out, or at the very least, in real trouble. Rhonda may not find out about it for another six to 12 months but her boss's "off to a slow start" plants a seed of doubt that could eventually lead to an unhappy ending for Rhonda.

After all, senior leaders are hired to deliver results first and foremost, and it is assumed that the required intelligence, personality, and attitude come along with the package. So when that question is asked about your transition, you want the answer to be about specific results, or early wins.

Compare the previous answer with "Rhonda? Let me tell you about all the things she's gotten done."

In that scenario, Rhonda's made it. Of course, she has not done it all herself. Her team has. But Rhonda got the team focused on delivering early wins and by doing so gave her boss something concrete to talk about.

Early wins give the leader credibility and provide the team confidence and momentum—three very good things. For NASA and Apollo 13, fixing the oxygen problem was the early win that made the entire team believe it could succeed and gave it the confidence to deal with the rest of the challenges and the momentum to push forward despite incredible odds.

The early win prescription is relatively simple:

1. Select one or two early wins from your milestones list:

   Choose early wins that will make a meaningful external impact.

   Select early wins that your boss will want to talk about.

   Pick early wins that you are sure you can deliver.

   Choose early wins that will model important behaviors.

   Pick early wins that would not have happened if you had not been there.

2. Jump-start early wins by Day 60 and deliver by your sixth month:

   Early means early. Make sure that you select and jump-start early wins in your first 60 days that you and the team can deliver by the end of your sixth month. Select them early. Communicate them early. Deliver them early.

Make sure that the team understands the early wins and has bought into delivering them on time.

This will give your bosses the concrete results they need when someone asks how you are doing.

3. Overinvest resources to ensure that early wins are achieved on time:

Do not skimp on your early wins. Allocate resources in a manner that will ensure timely delivery. Put more resources than you think you should need against these early opportunities so that your team is certain to deliver them better and faster than anyone thought was possible.

When asked what he would have done differently during his time in the White House, former U.S. president Jimmy Carter referred to the botched raid to rescue American hostages in Iran.

"I wish I'd sent one more helicopter to get the hostages, and we would have rescued them, and I would have been reelected."[3]

Stay alert. Adjust quickly. As the leader, stay close, stay involved in the progress of your early wins, and react immediately if they start to fall even slightly offtrack or behind schedule.

Send one more helicopter.

4. Celebrate and communicate early wins:

As your early wins are achieved, celebrate the accomplishments with the entire team. This is important and should not be overlooked.

In conjunction with your communication campaign, make sure that your early wins are communicated as appropriate.

In general, *early wins* are not synonymous with *big wins*. They are the early, sometimes small, yet meaningful wins that start the momentum of a winning team. They are the blasting caps, not the dynamite. They are the opening singles, not the grand slam home run. They are the first successful test market, not the global expansion. They may be found generally by accelerating something that is already in progress instead of starting something new.

Finally, they are sure to generate credibility, confidence, momentum, and excitement. Remember the watchers? The people who have not shown themselves to be detractors, yet, have also not stood

---

[3] 2015, press conference, Atlanta, August 20.

up as strong contributors. Once early wins begin, some of the watchers will edge closer, and eventually will jump in as contributors. After all, everybody wants to be part of the winning team, right?

Use Early Wins to Prove the Benefits in a Postmerger Integration

Michael was excited about an opportunity created by a recent acquisition that he had participated in and strongly supported. The belief was that the two companies' products, when packaged together, would represent a "total solution," which would command premium pricing and higher volumes.

To implement the total solution product, a new selling process needed to be developed and implemented. However, despite his efforts Michael had been unable to get traction from either sales organization to make any changes and move toward the new integrated model. The team had even identified an early win as closing a piece of business from a major customer, within a month, by leveraging a new selling process and combining the benefits of the two products. But progress was slow and they were clearly in danger of not hitting the early win.

So Michael allocated more resources to the early win and put his top implementation team, consisting of players from both sides of the integrated company, to execute the changes needed to craft the total solution. He promised his support to help them remove barriers along the way. He challenged the coleaders to design a rough selling and service model that would deliver the first sale—and that could be refined and automated later—as opposed to insisting on a perfect design, which would have taken weeks to implement.

The team had its first total solution sale within three months. Michael led the celebration. Later, he leveraged the rough, manual processes to build a repeatable system that allowed the team to realize the promise of the acquisition.

Don't Wait Too Long to Build Momentum

Adrienne had a bias to be accommodating to the people whom she worked with. Not that this is a bad thing per se, but she fell victim to the thought that everyone's individual priorities were more important than the team's Burning Imperative. As a result, she allowed the team to finish individual priorities that were established before she joined and waited to schedule her imperative workshop until it was convenient for everyone. She then scheduled it in a time and place that minimized travel for everyone and limited it to a one-day session to minimize disruption to the team's routine. Everyone appreciated that.

The trouble was that the Imperative session didn't happen until she'd been in her new job more than 90 days. By then, three months of momentum had been allocated toward the goals defined by the previously failed leader. The team members had decided that Adrienne wasn't going to push them to do anything differently, so they continued along the same track and realized they didn't have to take her initiatives seriously.

Held so late in her tenure, the team's Imperative session had no urgency and was rushed through without delivering any meaningful value. The team appreciated that it was minimally intrusive to members' schedules and left the meeting with the same individual priorities they had before Adrienne started. When she tried implementing a milestone-tracking process to track the delivery of the few new goals they defined in the meeting, the team protested that the process took too much time from day-to-day priorities, and it never took hold.

By being overly accommodating, bowing to existing priorities defined by someone else, dragging her feet on the Burning Imperative session, and failing to implement a rigorous milestone-tracking process, Adrienne guaranteed that she'd be delivering more of the same.

Focus on the Results with the Most Impact

Pamela came into lead sales and marketing for a struggling software provider. She knew that the product was very strong and well priced, but the company had little market penetration because of its less-than-stellar marketing efforts. Immediately on joining, Pamela co-created with her team a compelling Burning Imperative and the resulting strategies, plans, and milestones. Her team's important milestones included redoing the marketing strategy, positioning, branding, brochures, and trade show booth.

As an early win, she and the team picked redesigning the trade show booth and the trade shows strategy. Her logic was that there was a major trade show coming up in a few months and this was a great chance to make a powerful impact on the market. She knew that if the team was successful, the end result would be a significant increase in client interest and inquiries. If she could increase client requests for proposals, she knew fortunes would turn around because the sales team had an excellent close ratio once it got on a client's radar. By generating more client requests, she knew she would gain credibility for the marketing group, gain confidence for her team, and give senior management some meaningful results to talk about.

She closely managed the project while effectively engaging her team along the way, and she delivered a superior product in record time. Pam's team came up with a concept that attracted key clients and then blew them away once they were there. The sales team gave more presentations during the trade show than they had in the previous eight months. Her team's early win generated tangible, effective, and exciting results. It was far better than what the team had achieved before, and it was clearly something they never would have accomplished without Pamela. It was a great early win!

HOT TIP

To qualify as an early win, the result must be something that would not have been accomplished without you taking the leadership role. If it would have been accomplished without you in the role, it is not significant enough to be considered an early win. The early win should signify to the team and the other stakeholders that something has changed for the better. However, it must be seen and felt as the team's win and not your personal win alone.

Champion the Champions

Oscar decided to focus his efforts on four projects. He reached into his organization to pick four champions to drive the projects and then gave them extra support and resources to ensure that they could deliver in their new roles.

Three of the projects produced early tangible results. One did not do so well.

But the three that did well were enough to turn the whole business around. The division that Oscar had been brought in to run had experienced declining sales for 24 months, and continued its downward trend during Oscar's first two months. However, as the early win projects started to deliver results, the downward trend stopped in month three with a 1 percent uptick. By month four, it was up 4 percent, and in month five, it was up 10 percent. It was clear to all that the successful delivery of the three early wins was behind the overwhelming jump in sales. That success bought Oscar more time to achieve a win on the fourth plan.

No one even bothered asking how Oscar was doing in month six. Everybody knew because the numbers told the story.

Redefine Success

Quincy did not like the early win concept at all. He had just become the new head of the music division of a major entertainment company that was looking to make a dramatic impact on the music industry and turn around years of declining sales. Quincy knew that the existing pipeline of artists could not deliver the sales punch that his bosses were looking for, and he was certain that it would take 12 to 18 months to deliver anything tangible. To him, delivering a meaningful early win in his first six months seemed impossible.

Then he rethought how he defined early wins. He borrowed the pipeline concept from pharmaceutical companies and created a recording pipeline. On Day One, the pipeline was near empty. But, by month six he had an exciting array of new artists signed and viable projects in the pipeline and could show senior management the new face of the music division as his measure of success. His early win was a pipeline of opportunities—showing tangible momentum toward a longer-term goal.

Charter the Team for the Win

For the early win to create a sense of confidence and momentum in the team, the team needs to drive the win. You, as the leader, can inspire and enable by directing, supporting, and encouraging the team in the process, but it can't be your win. It must be the team's win. Therefore, your role as leader is to set the team up for success and support its efforts. The team charter and its five components are useful in doing that. They are laid out here and in Tool 6.2.

1. Objective—What?

   Clearly and specifically define the early win.

   Use the specific, measurable, achievable, realistic, and time bound (SMART) goal format to define specifically the early win and the required components along the way.

   The goals must be tangible results.

2. Context—Why?

   Provide the information that led to the desired results of the early win. (Be sure to include customer requirements if they exist.)

   Explain the intent of the early win to ensure that team members understand the collective purpose of their individual tasks. Monitor and adjust along the way to achieve that purpose while minimizing unintended consequences.

   Clarify what happens next. Make sure that the team understands the follow-on actions to ensure that momentum is sustained after the win is delivered.

3. Resources—With what help?

   Ensure that the team has and can access all the human, financial, and operational resources needed to deliver the objective. (Remember, for an early win, you're going to overinvest in resources to ensure delivery.)

   Clarify what other teams, groups, and units are involved and what their roles are.

   Allocate resources in a timely manner to ensure delivery.

4. Guidelines—How?

   Clarify what the team can and cannot do with regard to roles and decisions.

   Lay out the interdependencies between the team being chartered and the other teams involved.

   Decide what essential data is needed to measure results.

   Provide frequent and easy access to required data.

5. Accountability—Track and monitor

Clarify what is going to get done by when by whom and how the team and you are going to track milestones so that you can know about risks in advance and can intervene well before milestones are missed.

Clarify command, communication, and support arrangements so that all know how they are going to work together.

Schedule regular updates.

Know the signs when course corrections or reevaluations are necessary.

Celebrate Early Wins and Significant Milestones along the Way

Tracking milestones is not a revolutionary business idea. However, the idea of using them as a team-building tool is new to most leaders and their teams. Royal Caribbean's chief executive officer (CEO), Richard Fain, fully appreciates the power of milestones and exemplifies how other leaders can use them to keep projects on track and recognize employee achievements.[4]

Richard's emphasis on milestones is not a surprise, because ship builders have been leveraging milestones' emotional impact for millennia. Shipbuilders celebrate "keel laying" as the formal start of construction, naming, stepping the mast (accompanied by placing coins under the mast for good luck), christening (accompanied by breaking a bottle of champagne over the bow), a whole range of trials, "sail away," hand over, and onboarding the new captain (the genesis of the term *onboarding*).

One of Royal Caribbean's big projects was the creation of a central gathering area on the ship *Oasis of the Seas*. This area—which is aptly named Central Park—is located in the middle of the ship and opens to the sky for five decks. To celebrate the design, it created a full-size model of part of this open space in the massive hangar-like building where parts of the ship were being built in Finland. Also, the company treated the whole team to an alfresco fine dining experience so they could celebrate the space.

---

[4] George Bradt, 2011, "Royal Caribbean's CEO Exemplifies How to Leverage Milestones," *Forbes*, March 23.

"It was a magical evening. . . . We were having a lovely cruise dinner in Finland (in early Spring—when it's still cold outside). . . . It made us all realize how special the space would be and that it was worthy of the effort to really make sure that not only was the overall space good, but that all the details were perfect."

Drive Operational Accountability: Summary and Implications

Milestones. Define them and begin tracking and managing them immediately. Compiling milestones is a waste of time if you do not have an efficient, effective, and clear process in place to track them. Use this process to establish and reinforce expected team norms in three steps:

1. Get milestones in place.
2. Track them and manage them as a team on a frequent and regular basis.
3. Implement a milestone management meeting process.

Tracking milestones can be particularly effective when you are merging teams or creating new teams—the process unites.

Early wins are all about credibility, confidence, and momentum. People have more faith in people who have delivered. You want your boss to have confidence in you. You want the team to have confidence in you and in themselves. Early wins will provide that confidence.

QUESTIONS YOU SHOULD ASK YOURSELF

Is everyone clear on who (roles) is doing what (goals), when (milestones), with what resources and decision rights?

Am I choosing my captains and my team members wisely?

Are we doing all we can to make sure that information and resources flow to where they need to go?

Is there a system in place to manage milestone achievement so I do not have to do it myself on an ad hoc basis?

Am I effectively using milestone management as a team-building tool?

Am I certain that all my milestones are on track? If so, how can I be sure? If not, why not?

Have I identified an early win that will accomplish all that it needs to in terms of solidifying my leadership and giving the team confidence?

Do I have confidence in the team's strategy and tactical capacity to deliver this win?

Am I certain that I have invested enough resources to accomplish the win?

Do I have a comprehensive plan to monitor and adjust to ensure an early win victory?

What is my message when we celebrate this win—are we celebrating the win itself, or rather, how we got there?

Additional Articles and Tools on www.onboardingtools.com

6A.1   BRAVE Meeting Management–Curating Meetings
6A.2   Strategic Selling
6A.3   BRAVE Creative Brief
6A.4   Senior Management Trip Planning

TOOL 6.1
Milestone Management*

Use this tool to manage milestone management meetings and to follow up on progress as a team.

Milestone Management Process

Leader conducts a weekly or biweekly milestone management meeting with his or her team.

Prior to Milestone Management Meetings

Each team member submits his or her updates.

Designated person compiles and circulates updated milestones in advance of the meeting.

At Milestone Management Meetings

First part of the meeting:

> Each team member gives a five minute update in the following format: most important wins, most important learnings, and areas where he or she needs help.

Midpoint of the meeting:

> The leader orders topics for discussion in order of priority.

Second part of the meeting:

> Group discusses priority topics in order, spending as much time as necessary on each topic.

(continued)

TOOL 6.1   Milestone Management (continued)

The remaining topics are deferred to the next milestone management meeting or a separate meeting. Key items are updated and communicated.

Milestones Tracking

Milestones (Priority Programs)	When	Who	Status (Green, Yellow, or Red)*	Discussion/ Help Needed

*Green means "on track," yellow means "lagging but will be made up," and red means "heading for a miss."

TOOL 6.2
Team Charter for Delivering Early Wins*

Use this tool for getting teams off to the best start on their way to an early win.

Objectives/Goals: Charge the team with delivering specific, measurable results.

Context

Information that led to objectives:

Intent behind the objectives:

What's going to happen after the objective is achieved:

Resources: Human, financial, and operational resources available to the team. Other teams, groups, and units working in parallel, supporting, or interdependent areas.

Guidelines: Clarify what the team can and cannot do with regard to roles and decisions. Lay out the interdependencies between the team being chartered and the other teams involved.

Accountability: Be clear on accountability structure, update timing, and completion timing.

TOOL 6.3
Problem Solving*

Use this tool to help facilitate problem solving.

1. Share **prereading** to let people think about the problem and potential solutions in advance. This prereading should include, at a minimum, the problem, the current best thinking, the context, and some potential options.

2. Start with the problem owner's **current best thinking**. (You'll need clarity around who is the problem owner and who is the decision maker.)

3. Decide whether the group will **discuss** the problem. If yes:

4. Answer **questions for clarification** (to help people understand context and current best thinking, not for them to comment on or improve the thinking—yet).

5. Highlight the most **positive** aspects of the current best thinking contributing to making it work.

6. Identify **barriers** keeping the current best thinking from working. (Get all the barriers on the table at the same time before working on any of them.)

7. Decide on the **most important barrier**.

8. Direct a **brainstorm** on the most important barrier with all participating, including the problem owner. Look for statements from the team members that might help remedy the barrier. Require statements to be in the *What you do is . . .* (WYDIS) format.

9. The problem owner considers and pulls together a **possible remedy** to that barrier. Test it with the group.

---

*Copyright © PrimeGenesis LLC. To customize this document, download Tool 6.3 from www.onboardingtools.com. The document can be opened, edited, and printed. This Tool was originally developed by PrimeGenesis partner Roger Neill.

TOOL 6.3   Problem Solving (continued)

10. **Choice**: If the possible remedy is not strong enough, continue to work on this barrier. If the remedy works, determine whether that is enough to solve the overall problem. If yes, move on to action steps. If not, work on the next most important barrier.

11. **Action steps**: Agree who gets what done, by when, now that this problem is solved.

CHAPTER 7

Strengthen the Organization

GET THE RIGHT TEAM IN PLACE BY DAY 70.

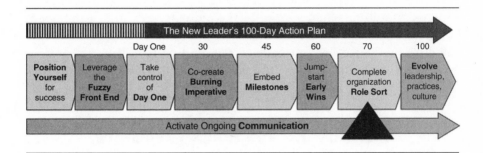

The New Leader's 100-Day Action Plan

Of all the tools in your toolbox, putting people in the right roles is one of the most powerful. It is also the most explosive. As you seek to evolve (or shock!) the culture, these moves will be the most decisive and will have the greatest impact.

Often, team members of a culture or organization that is beginning to evolve will watch and wait to see whether there are any consequences for not evolving with the new culture. They will pay particular attention to the team members who say things like, "All that meeting and report stuff is fine, but if it means I have to change what I do, forget it!" The moment somebody is terminated or moved or promoted, those who have been resisting the change often develop a completely different view of things. There is no single way to impact culture more quickly than changes to the organization.

Everybody on the team feels it when people moves are made. Everyone will have an opinion (usually strong) on the moves and how they affect him or her. Personnel moves spark emotions, fears, and egos, so you need to be thoughtful about who, what, and especially when you move people. Recognize that moving people should actually be seen as your most potent communication tool: This person means business and means it now!

As a leader, you can help your team and the people you're working with see their roles in a more comprehensive light if you make an effort to link them directly to their career development. Many people are not in the right role for the team's mission or even for their own professional development. Moving roles is often as much about doing what is right for the individual as it is for the team. If you can develop the leadership skill of communicating with people effectively about roles and careers, you will be investing not only in the success of your 100 days but also in your own long-term success as a leader.

The Structure and Roles Themselves Can Be the Cause of Problems

Keep in mind that not only will you inherit a team, but you will also inherit a structure and set of roles that might range from tightly defined to loosely implied. Don't make the mistake of assuming that the structure and roles are properly defined for what the group is trying to achieve. Often they are years old and were created for a mission that no longer exists. Take a step to eliminate ambiguity and clarify roles and responsibilities so they are clearly understood and precisely match the team's Burning Imperative. This is why you may want to wait until Day 70—by then, you have established your Burning Imperative (providing strategic context for structure and roles) and observed team members in action (providing context for matching individuals to roles).

Sometimes a team member is well suited for 90 percent of what's required in the role, but is seen as underperforming because he or she struggles with the 10 percent of the role that is not a match for him or her. Those elements of a role that are a significant mismatch for the person holding the role are *role outliers*. Role outliers are relative to the individual, not the role itself. They might make sense as a part of a greater role, but not when assigned to a particular individual as part of that role.

Sometimes role outliers can be revealed with one simple question: What's the least favorite part of your job? Listen to the answer, probe for more information, and you'll eventually uncover the obvious culprits. Find these and root them out. Assign those role outliers to others on the team who may be better suited to deliver against the requirement. Slight changes in role can have a dramatic impact on performance, levels of engagement, and satisfaction. Don't be afraid to be creative and avant-garde when redefining roles.

When Barry took over as chief executive officer of a marketing services company in London, he identified a need to improve the company's customer service capability dramatically. The company's ability to serve its customers had not kept up with the pace of innovation. The company had great products but poor customer service. This issue was identified and accepted as a priority by the team during the Burning Imperative workshop.

Responsibility for customer service sat with the vice president of sales, and despite positive intentions, he was unable to give the group the attention it required as its mission evolved. The customer service team was focused on *reacting* to queries, *not proactively* solving problems and ensuring strong usage and satisfaction. As the business evolved, fixes required input from others outside the customer service team. Cross-functional collaboration was required but the customer service team still needed to lead the way.

Given the urgency for better customer service, Barry carved the group out of sales and had them temporarily report directly to him. Immediately the team co-created enhanced customer service requirements and then restructured individual roles to ensure that the entire team was focused on delivering a far more proactive customer experience. Armed with new service objectives and enhanced role clarity, Barry appointed a committed team member to the new role of director of customer experience to lead the charge.

With a new focus on customer service objectives, greatly increased role clarity, and a leader focused on implementing, the team quickly made great strides in customer service and satisfaction. In addition, free from the burden of managing customer service, the sales leader was able to focus more of his time on developing a stronger sales organization, and sales began to increase.

A Framework for Planning

When it comes to sorting people and roles on your team, you need to work with a short-term and a long-term framework. Initially, you must look at your team to determine whether any short-term moves should be made—before Day One in a merger, by Day 70 in other cases. Then, in the longer term, you must continue to develop your team. This chapter deals with the shorter time frame. We'll go into more depth on some of the longer-term aspects in Chapter 8.

To accelerate both short- and long-term team development, think in terms of **A**cquiring, **D**eveloping, **E**ncouraging, **P**lanning, and **T**ransitioning talent (ADEPT). The headlines are in Table 7.1.

Structure and Roles

Start by defining the structure and set of roles that you need to realize your mission, execute your strategy, and deliver on your goals. The mission determines the makeup of the ideal organization over the long run. The resulting strategies and plans help determine what roles are required to do the things that need to be done on a daily basis. This gives you a map of the roles you need to have and the roles you may need to eliminate. This is also the time to root out the role outliers.

Table 7.1
ADEPT Framework for Talent Management

Acquire	Scope roles. Identify prospects. Recruit and select the right people for the right roles. Attract those people. Onboard them so that they can deliver better results faster.
Develop	Assess performance drivers. Develop skills and knowledge for current and future roles.
Encourage	Provide clear direction, objectives, measures, and so on. Support the resources and the time required for success. Reinforce desired behaviors with recognition and rewards.
Plan	Monitor people's performance over time. Assess their situation and potential. Plan future capability development, succession, and for contingencies.
Transition	Migrate people to different roles to fit their needs/life stage and company needs.

Southwest Airlines is in the business of transporting people by airplane. The organization needs to include people to maintain the planes, fly the planes, sell tickets, and service its passengers. It needs these roles. It does not need chefs, bartenders, or masseuses—even though some other airlines do have people in those roles.

Role Requirements

With a picture of ideal structure and roles in hand, you can now determine which roles will have the greatest impact on delivering against your mission, strategies, and goals. The roles responsible for these tasks are the critical ones. The other roles encompass tasks that can be done merely well enough. This is where strategy and people overlap. At this point you should determine which roles need to be best in class and invested in and which roles can be maintained or outsourced.

The airline industry has historically lost buckets of money over the long term. (This is true for most industries centered on transporting people.) Yet, Southwest makes money every year. Part of why it does is that it has figured out which are its critical roles. Southwest overinvests in maintenance roles so it can turn its planes around faster. It overinvests in training its stewardesses and stewards so passengers' in-air experience is fun. Conversely, it underinvests in food service and on-the-ground waiting spaces.

Right People in the Right Role

Now that you have defined the right structure and set of roles, and determined the requirements for success in those roles, it is time to see whether you've got the right people in the right roles (current) and who should be placed in new roles. It's unlikely that you'll acquire a team that is perfectly set up to deliver against your Burning Imperative. If you're lucky, with a couple of small tweaks you'll be on your way to a world-class team. However, depending on the amount of change that you are trying to drive, you may need to do a major overhaul. If so, be prepared for a lot of work and a lot of disruption. The earlier you make that assessment the better. Don't make the mistake of delaying or avoiding the people changes that need to be made while hoping that some magical transformation will occur. It won't.

For some reason, it is human nature to put off such decisions. Yet, the number one regret experienced senior leaders have is not moving fast enough on people. Have a strong bias for figuring the right role sort out as early as possible and making the moves quickly. Getting the right people in the right roles with the right support is a fundamental, essential building block of a high-performing team. Without the right people in the right roles, there is no team.

Getting the right people in the right roles is guided by the team's mission, vision, and values, as well as by individuals' strengths. Strengths are necessary for success. But they are not sufficient. People must want to do well and they must fit in. It is helpful to think in terms of strengths, motivation, and fit.

Strengths

Now, you are ready to match the right people with the right roles. Marcus Buckingham and Don Clifton's core premise is that people do better when they capitalize on their own individual strengths, which comprise talent, knowledge, and skills. According to Gallup, "a strength is the ability to consistently provide near-perfect performance in a specific activity. The key to building a strength is to identify your dominant talents, then complement them by acquiring knowledge and skills pertinent to the activity." Use a tool such as Gallup's Strength-Finders Assessment to help you better match talent to roles and as a valuable aid in career development for your team.[1]

Motivation

If you understand your people's values, your people's goals, and how they see what they are currently doing in light of those goals, you have a terrific advantage in helping them find or live up to the right role for themselves and for the organization. Look at recent performance reviews, go back to your journaling during your early days of onboarding (when you were developing your first impressions), and reflect on the observations you have made during your first weeks on the job.

Fit

Fit is determined by how well an individual's cultural preferences match with the organization's culture. Take a hard look at attitudinal perspective, values, and biases.

---

[1] Marcus Buckingham and Donald Clifton, 2001, *Now, Discover Your Strengths* (New York: Free Press).

Perspective is an attitude born out of how people have been trained to view and solve business problems. It is the accumulation of people's business experience as manifested in their mental models. People with a classic sales perspective may feel that they can sell any product to customers. Conversely, people with a marketing perspective may feel the organization should modify its products and services to meet customers' needs. It's not that one perspective is better than the other, just that they are different.

It is rare for all of any individual's values to match all of the organization's values. However, it is important for most of the core values to match and for none of them to be in direct conflict with each other.

Different people behave at work in different ways. Some roles may require people with a greater sense of urgency. Some roles require people who think things through thoroughly before jumping in. If someone who tends to get a later start on the day is assigned the role of generating overnight sales reports for the group before everyone else comes in, it would force the person to work in opposition to a natural bias and would most likely be a recipe for failure (and inaccurate reports!).

When Things *Aren't* Working, Don't Wait . . .

It is a classic tale. It was the seventh game of the 2003 American League Championship Series. The winner moved on to the World Series. The New York Yankees, perennial winners, and its pitching ace, Roger Clemens, versus the Boston Red Sox, with 86 years of disappointment and its pitching ace, Pedro Martínez.

Fourth inning: Clemens is struggling. Yankees manager Joe Torre takes him out—early, decisively, without much discussion.

Eighth inning: Martínez is struggling. Red Sox manager Grady Little goes out to the pitcher's mound and asks whether Martínez has "enough bullets in (his) tank."

The response: "I have enough."

Little leaves him in. "Pedro wanted to stay in there," Little said. "He wanted to get the job done, just as he has many times for us all season long."

As Martínez put it, "I would never say no. I tried hard and I did whatever possible to win the ballgame."

Martínez and the Red Sox proceed to blow the lead and lose the game. Once again Clemens, Torre, and the Yankees go on to the World Series whereas two weeks later, Little loses his job.

As the sportswriters put it, Little's decision was "based more on loyalty and emotion than logic."

From Torre's point of view, "In Game 7, you've got a short leash. I'd worry about his emotions after the game."

There is a lot in common between Game 7 and a complex transition. Everyone is on a short leash. So it's essential to move early, logically, and decisively.

. . . And, When Things *Are* Working, Stick with the Plan

Super Bowl history changed in 2015 on a single play stemming from perhaps the most damaging coaching call ever. The game was all but over. Seemingly, all the Seahawks had to do to win the game was give the ball one final time to Marshawn Lynch, their hard-charging, league-leading tailback.

With only 26 seconds left in the game and one yard from victory, Seahawk coach Pete Carroll ignored what had worked for his team all year. Despite the fact that the Seahawks were the best running team during the season, and Lynch had already gained more than 100 yards in the game, in his most crucial moment as coach, Carroll over-thought his move and didn't play to the team's strengths. He didn't hand the ball to Lynch. He didn't even fake to Lynch and have his nimble quarterback scamper outside for a touchdown. Instead, with the game on the line, he called a pass play. It was intercepted. The Seahawks lost.

After the game Pete Carroll took full blame for the call and said, "We were throwing the ball really to kind of waste that play." "I hate that we have to live with that."

As a leader, it's never sound strategy to waste a play or temporarily lose your identity and ignore what got you there.

Meanwhile, on the other side of the ball, Malcolm Butler, the Patriots' rookie cornerback, admitted he had been beaten on the same play during practice and was told by coach Bill Belichick, "You gotta be on that." Belichick did not call a time-out to devise a new strategy or insert new players. He trusted his well-trained players on the field to execute, regardless of how Seattle played it. Butler anticipated the play and after the game, said, "Memorization came through. . . . I jumped the route. . . . I just did my job."

With one horrible decision, the Seahawks lost their chance to win the Super Bowl. By sticking with who got them there and what they were trained to do, the Patriots emerged as winners. Again.

Don't Let One Bad Apple Spoil the Batch

Charlie was the new head of the division. One of his direct reports, Jack, was deploying blatantly passive-aggressive tactics to undermine Charlie's authority.

On a regular basis, Jack would:

Sit in the back of large meetings and carry on side conversations during Charlie's presentations.

Refuse to work on the agreed divisional priorities until he and his team had completed their annual plans presentation.

Refuse to do prework for Charlie's meetings because he didn't think the process was meaningful.

When it was suggested it was time to remove Jack from the team, Charlie responded, "Can't do it. My boss put Jack in place and I'm reluctant to make a move with someone he hired. I'll just work around him."

"If you remove Jack, there is a chance that your boss will think less of you as a manager because you didn't give Jack a chance. But, if you do not move on Jack, you will get fired within six months because Jack is going to make sure your team does not work."

Charlie removed Jack and filled the role with someone who was openly committed to the team's Burning Imperative. Six months later, Charlie's team had delivered on its early wins and was on schedule to deliver on its stated objectives. Charlie's boss commented on the high level of team unity, focus, and morale. He made no mention of Jack.

This story and the story of the Red Sox beating the Yankees in the American League Championship Series make the same point. You have to do what is right for the organization and what's right for the individuals. You have to find a way to get the right people in the right roles at the right time. You have to do it early and decisively. You should be aware and respectful of their emotions—but never let them interfere with making the right decisions at the right time.

Keep People in the Right Roles

Iris was promoted from chief operating officer (COO) to president of her division. One of her first moves was to move someone into her old role. For that job, she selected Jamil, who had been doing an excellent job as the head of technology. Over the years of working with Jamil, Iris felt he was intelligent, possessed great people skills, and was completely reliable. She assumed he'd be a natural for the COO role.

After promoting Jamil to the COO position, she also asked Jamil's top technology person, Rita, to assume the now vacant head of technology role. Initially Iris was quite pleased with the new team composition and felt confident in her potential for success. However, within the first 30 days as she worked with her team to co-create a new Burning Imperative, she started to see that Jamil was failing miserably because he was totally unaccustomed to the more consensual decision making of senior management. He was struggling to adjust and causing friction among the other team members. Meanwhile, Rita had continued going about her job as if nothing had changed and was ill equipped to handle her new management responsibilities. As a result, the technology team made several costly mistakes, something that had never happened under Jamil's leadership.

Iris was faced with a tough decision: admit that her first moves were a mistake, or try to live with the wrong people in the wrong roles. She needed to move quickly and correct the mistake. Living with the wrong people in such crucial roles would have been certain disaster. Convinced, Iris made the difficult choice to reorganize again. She quickly found a seasoned COO to run the division operations. She moved Jamil back into a technology role with a new title and added responsibilities that she knew he could handle, and Rita was relieved of her management responsibilities. It was a painful retrenchment in the short term, but the realignment quickly produced benefits for the entire team. The team appreciated Iris's willingness to correct her own mistakes for the betterment of the team.

Cut the Pain Out Early
(or, at Least, as Early as Practical)

Sherman had just taken over as general manager. He knew he had to improve both the sales and marketing functions dramatically, as soon as he could. To achieve that, he knew that he had to replace the heads of both functions, but he also knew that both were extremely valuable, respected employees who could make important contributions in other roles that would better leverage their strengths, motivation, and fit.

So Sherman began searching for their replacements immediately, while being open with them about what he was doing. He worked closely with them early on to build strong personal relationships with them and let them know that they were still of value to the organization, but that their roles would change to better fits within the changing organization.

Six months later, Sherman hired new heads of sales and marketing. He assigned the previous leaders as direct reports, but he put them in new, more appropriate roles that enabled them to make an important impact on the organization and actively helped their replacements succeed.

How Fast Should You Move on the Team?

In general, have your plan in place to sort roles and make people moves at the end of 70 days or 10 weeks. There will be times when you need to move much faster and times when it will take you longer to implement the plan, but the seventieth day is a good target time frame to have it all figured out.

There is a risk in moving too fast. The risk is that you'll make poor decisions and come across as too impulsive. By the seventieth day, you will have had a chance to see people in the Burning Imperative workshop, in the milestone management process, and for some of them, in the pursuit to deliver on an early win. By Day 70, you should have enough information to make those crucial decisions.

There's a larger risk in moving too slowly. At about 100 days, you own the team. Once you own the team, the problem children become your problem children. You can't blame the team's failings or unresolved issues on your predecessor anymore. Also, the other team members know who the weak links are, and they might have known since before you took the helm. They will want you to make the tough moves. The number one thing high performers want is for management to act on low performers so the whole group can do better.* If you move too slowly, the other team members will wonder what took you so long.

To be clear, you may not be able to implement your decisions all at once. You may need to put in place transition plans that support weaker team members or keep strong team members in the wrong roles during the time it takes to get their replacements on board and up to speed. It's not that you should make all your moves in your first 70 days, no matter what. But you should have the plan in place and begin making moves as appropriate and do so with a bias toward making the moves sooner rather than later.

A Pivotal Leadership Moment

Jeng-li knew he had a problem with his lead general counsel, Susanna. Her communication and management style along with her negative attitude and questionable values created a work environment that was far from what Jeng-li and the rest of his management team were trying to instill in the organization. However, he hesitated to do anything about it because he was worried how she might react and the resulting fallout. It turned out that everyone else on the management team was uneasy around Susanna, too. Eventually things got so bad that he could no longer avoid the problem. So he called in the corporate human resources (HR) people, and together they mapped out the plan to transition Susanna out of the organization.

Jeng-li scheduled a meeting with Susanna for four o'clock the next afternoon. At that meeting he and the corporate HR person presented the transition plan to Susanna, and she was immediately escorted out of her office. Susanna had sensed the moment coming and left without incident.

Having successfully kept the transition plan under wraps until the last moment, Jeng-li knew that the news would get out quickly after the conversation with Susanna. He wanted to be the one to tell people what he had done and why. So, knowing that everything communicates (including the order in which people are communicated to), he

---

*Thank you, Dave Kuhlman of Sibson Consulting, for this insight.

thoughtfully planned whom he would communicate to, when he would do it, and in what order. Immediately after his meeting with Susanna he told, in order:

1. His direct reports.
2. Susanna's direct reports.
3. Susanna's key contacts at the law firms that supported the division.

Then, on Monday morning he sent an e-mail out to the broader organization.

In his messaging, he made a specific decision not to position Susanna's departure as being for personal reasons or the like. He made it clear that Susanna was being terminated because she was hurting the organizational culture. It was one of the strongest statements Jeng-li could make on the importance of organizational culture. He took action to preserve the desired culture, he was honest about why he did it, and he communicated quickly and clearly to everyone who needed to know. His approach was well received and greatly appreciated, and it served to reinforce his personal values and the stated values of the team.

HOT TIP

Move faster on the team: Have a bias to move faster on your team than you think you should. The risks of moving too fast are nothing compared with the multiplier effect of leaving people in the wrong place too long. The number one thing that experienced leaders regret is not moving faster on their people.

Using Role Sort to Accelerate Change in Postmerger Integration

As described in Chapter 2, in a postmerger/acquisition situation, it is important to perform an initial role sort, to give clarity to team members around roles, responsibilities, and reporting lines—before Day One. By no means is it necessary to redesign the entire organization at that early stage—but it *is* critical to let people know what the change means for them (in the immediate term) and let them know that the organization will evolve over the ensuing few weeks and months as the team learns and the shared imperative is developed.

By Day 70, you should be in a position to declare (at least to yourself and your boss/board) a new structure, with clarity on roles and responsibilities and a strong point of view on who will be in which role. Implementation of the new structure can be phased in as quickly or as deliberately as the situation calls for.

Frank used the forcing mechanism of the role sort to create a new role called vice president of innovation a couple months into an integration and named an executive from the acquired business to lead the new function. This served two purposes—(1) created clear accountability around an area (new product development) that was critical to the success of the merger and (2) recognized an executive from the acquired team for his strengths and for the values and motivation he had demonstrated during the transition.

Map Performance and Role

Putting the right people in the right roles is a key driver of success. The heart of Tool 7.1 is a grid that matches people with roles. The grid is based on two dimensions: performance and role appropriateness. Mapping people on this grid then helps inform decisions about which people are in the right roles and which are in the wrong roles, so you can support some and move others. This is a simple but highly effective tool for thinking about a complex subject.

The performance measure is drawn from an individual's last or current review/assessment in his or her current role. It is driven by results versus goals and supplemented with recently observed performance, behaviors, and communication.

The role match measure is a correlation of the strengths, motivations, and fit required for the role compared with the strengths, motivations, and fit of the person filling that role. The role's strengths, motivations, and fit should be drawn from position descriptions. The individual's strengths, motivations, and fit could be drawn from his or her latest review, Gallup's StrengthFinder, or another assessment questionnaire or tool.

Keep in mind that some people may be in the wrong role precisely because they have outgrown it and are ready for a promotion. If you

FIGURE 7.1   Performance versus Role Match

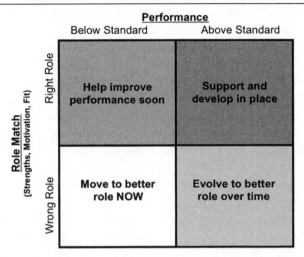

leave these people in their roles, you'll face a growing risk for decreased motivation. If there is an indication that an individual is struggling to make up for a mismatch between personal strengths and those required for the job, it is also a sure sign of a wrong role for that person (see Figure 7.1). Evolving is the appropriate action for these people. In either situation, the value of having a plan to move each candidate to a more appropriate role is clear. Delay those moves and you'll find yourself and your team in trouble.

In general, the suggested actions from Figure 7.1 are:

Support: Right Role/Above Standard: Keep these people in their current roles. Support and develop them. These people are helping and will continue to help. Stretch them, and make sure to push their ability to do good for others and for themselves as high as possible.

Improve: Right Role/Below Standard: Invest to improve these people's performance. They may be able to deliver with the right direction, training, and support. If they don't improve after support efforts, it may be a sign that they have reached their peak potential and therefore are in the wrong role.

Evolve: Wrong Role/Above Standard: Actively look for better fit before performance drops. Resist the temptation to keep them in their current role. They are helping, but the potential exists for even more.

There is also potential for flight as they become frustrated being in a role that is not right for them.

Move: Wrong Role/Below Standard: Quickly move them to a better role inside or outside the team.

Mapping performance and role appropriateness facilitates a more urgent identification of who is in the right role and who is in the wrong role now. It is important not to confuse *role match* with *potential* because there is a significant difference between the two.

Potential gets at future promotions. What is required to help people move up the ladder? What is the appropriate timeline for those promotions?

Role match gets at the current position. What's the likelihood of their performing well in their current position?

Every organization has its own way of doing position profiles. The better profiles include the key elements of the mission, vision, strengths, motivation, and fit. One way to do this is to answer the following questions in each of the following areas drawn from the recruiting brief—Tool 7.2 below.

Mission

Mission gets at what you expect out of the position.

What is the mission for this position? Why does it exist?

What are the responsibilities associated with the role?

What are the desired objectives or outcomes of the position?

What impact should the role have on the rest of the organization?

Vision

What is the picture of success?

How will things look when the mission is accomplished?

Strengths

Strengths include the talents, knowledge, and skills required to deliver the position's mission.

What talents are required to achieve success in the role? (Consider talents a recurring pattern of thoughts, feelings, or behaviors that can be productively applied.)

What knowledge is required to achieve success in the role? (Consider what the role holder needs to be aware of or know. What are the required education, experience, and qualifications?)

What skills are required to achieve success in the role? (Consider skills the how-tos, or the steps, of an activity. They can also be identified as capabilities that can be transferred, such as technical, interpersonal, or business skills.)[2]

Motivation

Motivation is what will drive the person in the role to succeed.

How do the activities of the role fit with the person's likes, dislikes, and ideal job criteria?

How will the person progress toward the long-term goal? What will drive him or keep her focused?

Fit

Fit refers to the match between the person's character and the culture he or she will be operating in.

Do the person's behaviors, way of relating to others, attitudes, values, and preferred working environment fit well with those of the organization?

Do the person's behavior, way of relating to others, attitudes, values, and preferred working environment fit well with those of the team?

Do the person's behavior, way of relating to others, attitudes, values, and preferred working environment fit well with those of the leader?

Developing Future Capabilities

As you begin to evolve the organization, keep in mind the three types of leaders: artistic, scientific, and interpersonal—and which type is the best fit in each role.

---

[2] The strengths definitions are drawn from Buckingham and Clifton's (2001) *Now, Discover Your Strengths* (New York: Free Press).

Table 7.2
Artistic, Scientific, and Interpersonal Leadership Characteristics

	Interpersonal	Scientific	Artistic
Where to play?	Context	Problems	Media
What matters/why?	Cause	Solutions	Perceptions
How to win?	Rally team	Better thinking	New approach
How to connect?	Hearts	Minds	Souls
What impact?	Actions	Knowledge	Feelings

When people see or hear *leader*, they generally think of inter-personal leaders inspiring and enabling teams. Although those inter-personal leaders are of critical import, the world needs artistic leaders and scientific leaders just as much. The common characteristic of all leaders is that they inspire others to become better than they would on their own. Each of the three types of leaders inspire others in different ways as described below and summarized in Table 7.2: Artistic, Scientific and Interpersonal Leadership Characteristics.

Artistic leaders inspire by influencing feelings. They help us take new approaches to how we see, hear, taste, smell, and touch things. You can find these leaders creating new designs, new art, and the like. These people generally have no interest in ruling or guiding. They are all about changing perceptions.

Scientific leaders guide *and* inspire by influencing knowledge with their thinking and ideas. You can find them creating new technologies, doing research and writing, teaching, and the like. Their ideas tend to be well thought through, supported by data and analysis, and logical. These people develop structure and frameworks that help others solve problems.

Interpersonal leaders can be found ruling, guiding, and inspiring at the head of their interpersonal cohort whether it's a team, organization, or political entity. They come in all shapes and sizes, and influence actions in different ways. The common dimension across interpersonal leaders is that they are leading other people.

Ask yourself, What type of leader does your team need the most, in each role? Is there a certain type of leader that is needed but not yet on the team? Evaluate all team members on their leadership potential and their natural type, and you'll start to find valuable clues on how to best develop them for continued success. One hallmark of the strongest leaders is their ability to develop other leaders along the way. The world needs more inspirational leaders, whether they are artistic, scientific, or interpersonal. Develop as many as you can along the way. The world will notice, and you'll leave a lasting legacy on your organization that will deliver consistent growth and inspire many lives.

Strong Performers and the *Three Goods*

Invest in your strong performers first. Way too many leaders get sucked into spending so much time dealing with underperformers that they don't pay enough attention to the people in the right roles performing particularly well until those people walk in to announce they're leaving.

Of course by then it's too late. Counteroffers almost never work.

Instead, treat your strong performers so "good" all along the way that they will not ever be open to the conversation about possibly leaving. Remember this is actually three goods:

1. *Good for others:* Inspire your strong performers with the *good for others* part of your mission or purpose.
2. *Good at it:* Do what it takes to remove any barriers that hinder your strong performers' ability to do more of what they are good at.
3. *Good for me:* Ensure your strong performers receive the recognition and rewards they deserve. As your strong performers' knowledge, skills, and accomplishments grow, make sure the person recognizing and rewarding their new market worth is you.[3]

Strengthen the Organization:
Summary and Implications

Put in place organizational processes to acquire, develop, encourage, plan, and transition (ADEPT) talent over time.

The mission, vision, objectives, and strategies inform the ideal organizational structure and help identify the required roles.

---

[3] George Bradt, 2015, "Why You Should Never Make or Take Counter Offers," *Forbes*, November 11.

The vision helps define role requirements, including which roles are required to be best in class.

In filling roles, match performance, strengths, motivation, and fit of individuals to the role:

Support and develop high performers in right roles.

Improve performance of low performers in right roles.

Evolve high performers in wrong roles to better roles over time.

Move low performers in wrong roles to better roles now.

Some of your most painful choices are going to be in this area. Trying to please everybody will lead to pleasing nobody. Choosing to act on people who are in the wrong roles now or will soon be in the wrong roles is generally not the most enjoyable part of leadership. But it is an essential part.

QUESTIONS YOU SHOULD ASK YOURSELF

Am I moving at the right speed to get the right people in the right roles?

Have I defined the right organizational structure and set of roles?

Have I defined the requirements for the specific roles properly?

Have I evaluated every team member on strength/motivation/fit versus role requirements?

Am I making the tough choices on people as soon as I have identified a mismatch?

Am I considering the right balance of leadership skills and styles on my leadership team?

Do I have adequate development plans in place?

Do I have appropriate backup and contingency plans?

Do I have the right organizational processes in place for the longer term?

Am I creating an environment where future leaders are encouraged to emerge and develop?

Additional Articles and Tools on
www.onboardingtools.com

TOOL 7.1
Role Sort*

Performance

	Below Standard	Above Standard
Right Role	Help improve performance soon	Support and develop in place
Wrong Role	Move to better role NOW	Evolve to better role over time

Role Match (Strengths, Motivation, Fit)

People Actions

Right Role/Above Standard: Keep in current roles. Support and develop them. These people are helping and will continue to help. Make sure to push their compensation, employability, meaning in the work, and share in shaping of their maximum potential.

Right Role/Below Standard: Invest to improve these people's perform-ance. They can deliver with the right direction, training, and support.

Wrong Role/Above Standard: Actively look for better fit before performance drops. Resist the temptation to keep them in their current role. They are helping, but the potential exists for even more.

Wrong Role/Below Standard: Quickly move to a better role inside or outside the team.

---

* Copyright © PrimeGenesis LLC. To customize this document, download Tool 7.1 from www.onboardingtools.com. The document can be opened, edited, and printed.

TOOL 7.2
Recruiting Brief*

Recruit for job title, department, compensation grade, start date.

Mission/Responsibilities

Why position exists

Objectives/goals/outcomes

Impact on the rest of the organization

Specific responsibilities

Organizational relationships & interdependencies

Vision (picture of success):

Strengths

Talents—inherent

Knowledge—learned (education, training, experience, qualifications)

Skills—practiced (technical, interpersonal, business)

Motivation

How activities fit with person's likes/dislikes/ideal job criteria

How to progress toward long-term goal

Fit

Behaviors, relationships, attitudes, values, environmental preferences

Work style, characteristics—company's

Work style, characteristics—group's

Work style, characteristics—supervisor's

CHAPTER 8

Keep Building

EVOLVE YOUR LEADERSHIP, PRACTICES, AND CULTURE TO DELIVER RESULTS.

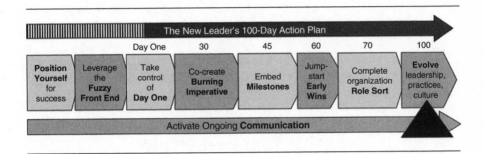

Y ou have reached the 100-day mark. You put a plan in place, leveraged your Fuzzy Front End to learn quickly, refined your plan, and developed solid relationships with all of your key stakeholders. You engaged the culture and made a strong early impression by delivering a clear message to your new audiences (up, down, and across). Your team is energized by its co-created Burning Imperative. You have established a milestone management process to drive accountability and are beginning to deliver early wins. Your team is in place.

So, what's next? Keep going. Keep building. Begin the process of continual evolution. You'll want to evolve in three key areas:

1. **Leadership:** The 100-day mark is a good moment to *gain feedback on your own leadership* during the first 100 days, so you can

determine *what* you should keep, stop, and start doing—and *how*—to be even more effective with your team and the organization as a whole.

2. **Practices:** From there, it is an opportune time to decide how you are going to *evolve your practices* to capitalize on changing circumstances. You should focus on practices that relate to people, plans, performance tracking, and program management.

3. **Culture:** Finally, after 100 days, your insights on the culture are sharper than when you started. You are also clearer about where you want to *evolve the culture*. Now is time to zero in on the biggest gaps and implement a plan to create and maintain the winning culture that will become your greatest competitive advantage.

By evolving your own leadership, your practices, and your culture, you are setting yourself up to deliver better results—not only faster but also sustainably, over time.

Evolve Your Leadership

Take a three-step approach to evolving your leadership. First, assess your effectiveness as a leader, defining specific areas you need to adapt to be more effective. Second, prepare a concrete leadership development plan that specifies not only *what* to focus on to drive results, but also *how* you need to be communicating with and leading the members of your team to drive engagement. And, third, identify a support partner to help you refine your plan and stay on track.

Start with self-assessment. Refer to whatever documents you have available—your original 100-day plan, your milestone management document, or your recent financial results—and assess how you have performed so far versus the goals that you (and your board and your boss) set. Rate yourself green if you are on track, yellow if you are at risk (yet have a solid plan to get back on track), and red if you will miss (and do not have a solid plan to get back on track).

Next, have someone collect 360-degree feedback on your performance from your critical stakeholders up, across, and down. (Answer the same questions yourself so you can compare your own thoughts to others'.) Doing this will help you (1) see how others feel, (2) highlight disconnects between how you and others see you, and

(3) model the behavior of seeking and considering personal input from others. Questions:

- What is it that the new leader does that is particularly effective? What should he or she *keep* doing?
- What does the new leader do that gets in the way of his or her effectiveness? What should he or she *stop* doing?
- What else could the new leader do to be even more effective? What should he or she *start* doing?

Now, you are ready for leadership development planning. With the outputs from the self-assessment and 360-degree feedback processes, you have a list of items to consider as you create your own development plan. Bracket them into key deliverables (across strategic, operational, and organizational matters) and key leadership habits in terms of the behaviors you need to strengthen to become even more effective.

It is likely the items that emerge during your self-assessment and 360-degree feedback processes are ones that you know how to manage. You'll understand the feedback, the actions, the changes, and the adjustments that are required to evolve to where you need to be. In many cases, for both key deliverables and key leadership habits, you may benefit from having a partner to support your own development efforts.

You'll certainly want to invest in the relationship with your boss. Establish a rolling agenda with the right balance of fixed and changeable items, and establish a regular communication cadence. In addition to your boss, you will benefit greatly from finding a partner to support you as you build and implement your leadership development plan. The criterion? Someone you trust. This could be a mentor or former boss, a board member, your human resources partner, an external coach, or a consultant.

In any case, find the support to help you turn your desire into action and your action into habits. You will evolve and become an even better leader for the effort.

Evolve Your Practices

The 100-day mark is a good time to begin thinking about evolving your practices around people, plans, performance tracking, and program management. It's useful to set up a predictable rhythm. This allows people to spend less time worrying about the process and more time figuring out how to react and capitalize on the inevitable changes around them.

People

With your team members in consideration (and the strengths they bring and don't bring), you will want to align the longer-term organizational development plans with the longer-term (three-plus years) strategic plan. Look at four components:

1. *Future capability development planning* starts with the long-term strategy and then looks at what human capabilities you're going to need over time to be able to implement that long-term plan. That creates a future-state organizational plan. Compare that with your current-state organization to identify where the gaps exist between the two. Generally, you'll plan to close those gaps with a combination of:

   a. Developing your current people

   b. Acquiring people with new talents and developing them over time

   c. Acquiring people requiring less development closer to the time of need

   d. Acquiring people ready to go at the time of need.

2. *Succession planning* starts with the people you have in place in key roles and lays out who can take their places over time. Some of those potential successors may require development.

3. *Contingency planning* evaluates who can jump in and fill a position if one of your leaders can no longer do that for some reason. Some of these seat fillers may be permanent. Some may be on interim assignments. Some may be outsiders brought in for a short period.

   Do these three processes together on an annual basis.

4. *Performance management and talent review*

   Track progress of the longer-term future capability development plan and the corresponding talent needs. Monitor the progress of individual development plans, and help people maximize their potential by giving them training to build their knowledge and projects where they can practice and build skills.

   Do this annually.

Plans

Strategic Review, Refresh, and Plan

Conduct a detailed long-term look at the business (three-year horizon), leading to choices around how to create and allocate resources over that longer-term horizon. Relook at your Burning Imperative.

Do this annually.

Operational Review, Refresh, and Plan

Ensure the right operational plans (one-year horizon) that will enable you to deliver the next year's goals are in place.

Do this annually.

Performance Tracking

Business Reviews and Plan Updates

Track progress in the context of the operational plan (one-year horizon), and make midcourse adjustments along the way. Make certain you are aligned with your boss and board regarding the level of detail expected, areas of focus to be covered, and persons responsible for certain elements. Private equity firms often have a model that works for them across their portfolio companies, so you may need to adjust your model to meet their requirements.

Do this quarterly. See Tool 8.1.

Milestone Updates and Adjustment

Track the monthly milestones to keep the team focused on the most important deliverables, as a team.

Do this monthly, unless particular milestones are falling off target, in which case you should increase the frequency until the milestones are back on track.

Thinking about these things with these horizons allows you to have a good balance between long-term thinking and short-term execution. Many have blended these into an annual/quarterly/monthly meeting schedule. The idea is to have a meeting every month with time added once each quarter to deal with longer-term issues. It is a cycle with each piece feeding into the next. Use a calendar (Table 8.1) as a starting point, and then adjust it to meet your organizational needs without dropping any key pieces.

Table 8.1
Prototypical Quarterly Meeting Flow

Quarter	Month	Schedule
1	1	Milestone update and adjustment
1	2	**Business review and adjustment/Talent reviews**
1	3	Milestone update and adjustment
2	1	Milestone update and adjustment
2	2	**Business review and adjustment/Strategic review and planning**
2	3	Milestone update and adjustment
3	1	Milestone update and adjustment
3	2	**Business review and adjustment/Future capability, succession, and contingency planning**
3	3	Milestone update and adjustment
4	1	Milestone update and adjustment
4	2	**Business review and adjustment/Operational review and planning**
4	3	Milestone update and adjustment

Program Management

As a new leader, whether you are replacing an incumbent in an existing role or stepping into a new one created by a merger, acquisition, or reorganization, you are likely being asked to transform your organization and take performance to a higher level in a period that is much shorter than you may be accustomed to (particularly if you are operating in a private equity–owned or venture capital–owned environment).

As a result, it is likely there will be several new projects being introduced to the team, all with the objective of creating value. They might be projects to drive innovation, sales effectiveness, expense reduction, or operational excellence; benchmark human capital needs; upgrade systems; upgrade teams; or identify alliance partners and merger and acquisition targets. Whether you inherit or introduce these new value-enhancing projects during your Burning Imperative, you will begin to have a feel for the organization's ability to absorb the amount of change you wish to drive and the number of new projects coming on board at the same time. If the number of initiatives is overwhelming, and it probably will be, you can increase team capacity by introducing a program management expert or capability.

Program management is the process of managing several related projects, often with the intention of improving the organization's performance. The benefit of a program management skill set on the team is the ability to look across multiple projects for dependencies, bottlenecks, resourcing issues, and time conflicts. A strong program manager can identify challenges, bring choices into the light, and enable decision making by the team. For some new teams, managing one or two new projects in addition to daily responsibilities is plenty complex. Imagine when multiple projects, not to mention large ones like acquisitions, are introduced. Chaos ensues!

You may find program management skill sets already reside in your organization—likely places to look are information technology (IT), operations, finance, strategy, and product development. If you do not have the requisite skills in-house, consider hiring full- or part-time program management experts to help you drive your transformation program.

See Tool 8.3.

Evolve Your Culture

Now that you are 100 days into your new role, it is a good time to implement steps to evolve the organization even more assertively to your target culture.

As described in the executive summary, think about the new leader's role in building culture as a five-phase process:

1. Identify your cultural preferences (Prepare yourself for success).

   At this stage you evaluated the degree of cultural fit from your perspective, before accepting and starting the job.

2. Observe the organization's defined and undefined cultural identity (Leverage your Fuzzy Front End).

   At this stage you purposefully gathered information to prepare yourself for the culture you were about to enter.

3. Craft your own cultural engagement plan (before Day One).

At this stage:

- You determined your level of assertiveness in entering the organization (shock, assimilate, or converge and evolve) based on your assessment of the organizational need for change versus its readiness for change.
- You identified your stakeholders as detractors, supporters, or watchers to help focus your relationship-building efforts.
- You built and refined your going-in messaging, reflecting the platform for change and call to action for the team.

4. Begin to influence and drive the culture during your first 100 days.

At this stage:

- You sent messages early and often signifying what was important to you (your values) by what you said and where and with whom you spent time.
- You co-created a Burning Imperative that was a huge step in defining the culture, by gaining alignment on mission, vision, values, strategies, actions, and operating cadence.
- You established a milestone management tool and pushed for early wins to set a cultural tone.
- You made decisions on people and structure and communicated them in a way to support changing the culture toward your vision.

5. Evolve the culture after Day 100.

Three-Part Approach

First, make sure you and your leadership team are aligned on the specific values and behaviors you are attempting to imbed into the culture.

Second, work with your leadership team to evaluate where you are as an organization against the dimensions of a culture: behaviors, relationships, attitudes, values, and the environment (BRAVE). Identify where you believe you need to focus as a team to move closer to the desired state.

Third, now that you and your leadership team are aligned on the BRAVE, and clear about where you need to evolve across those components, you can employ culture-shaping tools to embed the desired culture, over time.

Culture-Shaping Tools

There are many tools available to help you evolve your culture. A few that can make the greatest impact:

Performance Feedback and Reviews
Adapt your performance feedback and review process in a couple of ways. First, in the formal written process, be sure to include not only business goals that can be measured, but also an evaluation (including a numeric value) on the stated company behaviors and values. When providing feedback in this forum, be detailed and specific. Go out of your way to provide specific examples of culture-enhancing behaviors as well as culture-killing behaviors.

Informally, model a culture where constructive feedback is given and received in the spirit of individual and company improvement. Be ready to give feedback, both negative and positive, in the moment.

Reward and Recognition
Think of reward and recognition as the public version of positive feedback. Deploy a simple program that recognizes not only performance against business goals but also demonstration of culture-enhancing behaviors and values. At first, control the process so managers get a feel for what is deserving of recognition. Once you are confident the program will be applied consistently, allow managers and employees to recognize their peers and coworkers. More positive feedback will lead to more positive behaviors!

Communication
An active internal communications program is the lifeblood of a cultural evolution. First, get your messages clear, what you wish to reinforce about the culture you are driving. If people need to work more closely as a team to solve customer problems, institute a Lunch & Learn or similar program to share information and get on the same page. Or, encourage leadership team members to invite peers to their staff meeting to share news from their departments. If you are trying to evolve the team and the culture to a more aggressive posture in the market, celebrate wins where team members were assertive, took a risk, and won the business.

These efforts must evolve to capitalize on changing circumstances as well. With minor changes, your message may remain the same.

However, if the change is major, your message and touch points must be adjusted to match the new reality. In some cases, the change may be significant enough to warrant a complete revamping of the plan. Either way, make sure you are controlling your own message and how it is communicated.

The ideas will flow; just be sure you do map your messages to your audiences, and have a continuous and multimedia approach to communicating culture.

NOTE ON CULTURE

See Tool 1A.10 on www.onboardingtools.com for a discussion of culture across all the steps of onboarding. (Same material as in the book, just compiled into one document on BRAVE culture.)

Think Differently

Succeeding a legend is one of most difficult transitions a chief executive officer can make because the scrutiny is far more intense and every move is magnified. No one knows this better than Tim Cook, who took the role as Apple's CEO in 2011, following one of the most celebrated leaders of all time, Steve Jobs. Cook inherited a company that was on top of its game, with a strong culture that was forged by Jobs's dominant personality. Many assumed that Cook would mind the shop and change as little as possible, hoping to continue along the same path to success. But Cook realized that he could not run the company as Jobs had, because he wasn't Jobs.

Despite the company's astronomical success, Cook's first message upon coming on board was that "our best days are ahead of us." A bold statement that sent a signal to shareholders and customers that he expected to lead Apple to even greater success in the future.

First, to underscore stability, he signaled early on that he would keep most of the existing management team in place and that he would guard and defend the distinct Apple culture with vigor.

Cook then quickly gave the executive team more control over decisions. Under Jobs, the team had become used to a CEO management style that was overpowering and burdened with micromanagement.

Cook let team members know that his style was to be an active coach who inspires and trusts them to make more decisions on their own.

He then moved to make Apple more open by allowing his executives more freedom to speak with the press and outside the organization. He also shared the success spotlight outside the CEO's office.

He's also made Apple more reflective of its culture. A historically private and low-key leader, he decided to announce publically that he was gay in an effort to be more transparent himself and demonstrate leadership outside the organization. He's used the spotlight to speak out on other societal issues, many of which reflect important values held internally by Apple. Along the way he has donated millions to charity and has encouraged Apple employees to do so as well, a distinct departure from Jobs.

Cook has also changed Apple's growth and financial approach by using its large cash stores to complete large-scale buybacks of Apple stock, issue regular dividends to shareholders, make large-scale acquisitions, and bring some production back to the United States, all strategies that Jobs either opposed or avoided.

By keeping what worked and slightly adjusting in key areas that would better position Apple for the future, Tim Cook has been able to do what many thought was impossible—keep and improve upon Apple's momentum. Under his leadership, Apple's market capitalization has dramatically increased, worldwide market share has increased, and he's had two very successful product launches. His meaningful adjustments to an already-fantastic organization and culture have allowed Apple to continue to provide inspiration and deliver even better financial performance.

Adjust to the Inevitable Surprises

John Wooden, the legendary coach of University of California at Los Angeles (UCLA) basketball, whose teams won an astounding 10 U.S. National Collegiate Athletic Association championships, said: "Things turn out the best for the people who make the best of the ways things turn out." As a leader, it is up to you to make the best of how things turn out. No matter how well you have planned your transition over the first 100 days, no matter how disciplined you are in your follow-up, some things will be different than you expected. Often your ability to keep moving forward while reacting to the unexpected or the unplanned will

Table 8.2
Change Map

Type	Temporary Impact	Enduring Impact
Major change	**Manage**: Deploy incident management response plan	**Restart**: Requires a fundamental redeployment
Minor change	**Downplay**: Control and stay focused on priorities	**Evolve**: Factor into ongoing team evolution

be the determining factor in whether your transition is deemed a success or failure.

One of the main advantages to starting early and deploying the building blocks of tactical capacity quickly is that you and your team will be ready that much sooner to adjust to changing circumstances and surprises. Remember, the ability to respond flexibly and fluidly is a hallmark of a team with tactical capacity. The preceding annual/quarterly/monthly meeting schedule will enable your team to recognize and react to the changes that might impact your team over time.

Not all surprises are equal. Your first job is to sort them out to guide your own and your team's response. If it is a temporary, minor blip, keep your team focused on its existing priorities. If it is minor, but enduring, factor it into your ongoing people, plans, and practices evolution.

Major surprises are a different game. If they're temporary, you'll want to move into crisis or incident management. If they're enduring, you'll need to react and make some fundamental changes to deal with the new reality. When you're evaluating change, use Table 8.2 to help guide you to an appropriate measured response.

Major but Temporary

Major but temporary surprises start out either good or bad. They don't necessarily stay that way. Just as a crisis handled well can turn into a good thing, a major event handled poorly can easily turn into a serious crisis. The difference comes down to preparing in advance, implementing the response, and learning and improving for the next time.

1. Prepare in Advance

As the team leader, it is on your shoulders to prepare in advance for potential surprises by anticipating potential events and crises and having procedures in place to follow if those things happen. Be assured that crisis events will never unfold exactly as you have planned for them. It is less important that you are exactly right in identifying the particular crisis that might come your way, but most important that you and the organization or team have a response in place for unexpected events.

Think through the possible situations, your desired result, and the basic approach to get there. Then map out what is going to get done by when and by whom and how you are going to communicate with the stakeholders who are essential to implementing a successful response or those affected by the chosen response. Once your plans are in place, periodically review the response plan so you are ready to identify and react to surprises when they do hit. The better you have anticipated possible scenarios, the more prepared you are, the more confidence you will have when crises strike.

2. Implement a Response

The reason you prepared is so that you all can react quickly and flexibly to the situation you face. Don't overthink or overmanage this. Do what you prepared to do, and let others do what they prepared to do.

When the inevitable surprise happens, put in place a specific plan for that particular event or crisis, using your preplanned response as a starting point. Implement your response following the basic milestone management process. One important difference is that instead of running your milestone meetings on a monthly basis, you'll run them far more frequently. Depending on the crisis, you may want to consider running them daily, if not even more frequently. Most likely, you will want to keep them relatively brief and laser-focused and drive the team's time and efforts heavily toward the actual implementation of your crisis plan.

Once you start to see results and the crisis starts to become stabilized, do not make the mistake of pulling back your efforts too soon. Crises have a nasty habit of getting out of control because someone takes his or her eyes off the ball too soon. It is hard to know when the temporary event or crisis is completely over. So have a bias to stick with the follow-through longer than you might think is necessary.

3. Learn and Improve

Once the crisis is over, complete a comprehensive review of your organization's response across three key areas: preparedness (precrisis), response (crisis management), and prevention (post-crisis). In each area, identify the gaps in your organization's performance and find ways to rectify them.

- **Preparedness**—Was the team adequately prepared to respond to the current crisis and implement the response?

- **Response**—Did the team respond well and how can it improve its capabilities to respond to future crises?

- **Prevention**—How can the organization reduce the risk of future crises happening in the first place?

Once your gap analysis is complete, take the steps to implement the changes required to improve your ability to deal with the next crisis. There will be a next one.

Major and Enduring

Major changes that are enduring require a fundamental restart. These can be material changes in things such as customer needs, collaborators' direction, competitors' strategies, or the economic, political, or social environment in which you operate. They can be internal changes, such as reorganizations, acquisitions, or spin-offs; getting a new boss; or your boss getting a new boss.

Whatever the change, if it's major and enduring, hit a restart button. Go right back to the beginning; do a full situation analysis; identify the key stakeholders; relook at your message; restart your communication plan; and get your people, plans, and practices realigned around the new purpose. Remember, the fittest adapt best.

Keep Building: Summary and Implications

Your leadership: Assess your own leadership and put in place a plan to make it even better. Get support to implement that plan.

People: Invest in future capability development planning, succession planning, and contingency planning; performance management; and talent reviews annually.

Plans: Conduct strategic reviews, refreshes, and planning as well as operational reviews, refreshes, and planning annually.

Practices: Conduct business reviews and plan updates quarterly and milestone updates and adjustments monthly.

Program management: Invest in this skill set when the sheer volume of change is stretching the organization beyond its capacity to manage with existing processes.

Culture: Close the gap between today's culture and your target culture by engaging your leadership team and deploying tools that will reinforce and accelerate the change program.

Surprises: Adjust to the inevitable surprises based on the degree and length of their impact.

Finis origine pendet (the end depends on the beginning)—so says the first-century Latin poet Marcus Manilius. In a transition into a new leadership role or team merger, if you do not get the beginning right, the end will be ugly.

Conversely, if you follow this book's framework and take advantage of its advice and tools, you will lead your team to the right place, in the right way, at the right times. If you do this, you will develop trust, loyalty, and commitment—and your team will follow.

By using the proven onboarding methodologies presented in this book to enhance and synchronize your people, plans, and practices, you will build the tactical capacity to inspire and enable others to do their absolute best together, to realize a meaningful and rewarding shared purpose that delivers better results faster than anyone thought possible.

Additional Articles and Tools on www.onboardingtools.com

8A.1   Leading a Start-Up Team (less than 10 people)
8A.2   Leading an Extended Family Team (10-30 people)
8A.3   Adding Appropriate Hierarchy to a Larger Team (over 30 people)
8A.4   BRAVE Operating Principles for HATCHing a Better Team

TOOL 8.1

Quarterly Reviews*

Use this tool and its prototypical agenda to plan out your quarterly meeting cadence.

Topics: Financial results versus plan, prior year, and forecast and progress against key initiatives

Every quarter:

Prior Quarter Review: Results versus expectations and applicable learning

Current Quarter Update: Track progress and make tactical adjustments

Next Quarter Go: Confirm implementation details

Two Quarters out Set: Finalize plans

Three Quarters out Ready: Agree on preliminary plans

Four Quarters out Prep: Agree on priorities

Annual tasks to be covered during the quarterly review process:

Q1: Talent review

Q2: Strategic planning (three-year financial targets)

Q3: Future capability development, succession, and contingency planning

Q4: Next year's operating plans and budgets

TOOL 8.2
Internal Communications*

Use this tool to plan your internal communications.

Drive compliance with indirect communication to make people aware.

Encourage contribution with direct communication to help people understand.

Support commitment with emotional communication to fuel belief.

Indirect Communication (through relatively mass media and large-group meetings)

- Daily blog posts
- Weekly updates
- Monthly recaps
- Quarterly and annual reviews
- Special announcements as warranted

Direct Communication (small-group meetings to allow for questions and answers and discussion)

- Daily/Weekly/Monthly staff meetings
- Quarterly reviews
- Special meetings

Emotional Communication (one-on-one to get at emotions)

- Antecedents to prompt important behaviors
- Consequences of behaviors (positive and negative)

(continued)

TOOL 8.2   Internal Communications (continued)

Leverage the ABCDE model to optimize communication effectiveness:

A Audience: Determine which audience(s) you intend to reach.

B Behavior: Define the desired behavior from your audience (belief, understanding, commitment).

C Content: Craft the messages and specific content.

D Design: Determine manner, mode, and environment for the communication.

E Evaluation: Measure the effectiveness of the communication in driving the desired behavior(s).

TOOL 8.3
Program Management*

Use this tool to help with your program management.

Objectives/Goals: Specific, measurable results (SMART)

Context

- Information that led to the objectives
- Intent behind the objectives
- What's going to happen after the objective is achieved

Resources: Human, financial, and operational resources available to the team. Other teams, groups, and units working in parallel, supporting, or interdependent areas.

Guidelines: What the team can and cannot do with regard to roles and decisions. Interdependencies between the team being chartered and the other teams involved.

Accountability: Structure, update timing, and completion timing

Roles and Responsibilities (Responsible, Accountable, Consulted, Informed)

Milestone Tracking

Area	Task	Date	Person Responsible	Status/Update

TOOL 8.4

Coaching and Support*

Use this framework to evolve your leadership and potentially enter into a coaching/support relationship.

1. Begin with the end in mind: objectives, goals, end state
2. Understand current reality: the current state
3. Agree on strengths and barriers: what's working/causing the gap
4. Plan to bridge gaps: Attitude? Relationships? Behaviors?
5. Implement, monitor, adjust: changes and impact

Tactically:

Retrospective coaching: Situation? Action? Result? What worked well? What worked less well? Implications?

Prospective coaching: End in mind? Situation? Barrier/problem to solve? How to close gap/solve problem?

Tool:

Utilize 360-degree feedback or a more detailed diagnostic tool to determine areas for improvement

- Leverage trusted third party (HR, coach, consultant, mentor no longer in the same organization)
- Trusted third party engages and gains feedback from direct reports, peers, and boss(es)
- Seek feedback on areas to *keep*, *stop*, and *start* doing to increase effectiveness
- Debrief with third party and boss to determine areas of focus, actions, and coaching routine

---

TOOL 8.5
100-Hour Plan for Crisis Management*

Use this tool to prepare for and work through crises.

Organization's Purpose:

Update

Wins—Share and celebrate the good things that have already happened

Learning—Share learning that can help others

Help—Highlight areas needing more support

Physical, Political, Emotional, Reputational, Financial Context

What do we know and not know about what happened and its impact (facts)?

What are the implications of what we know and don't know (conclusions)?

What do we predict may happen (scenarios)?

What resources and capabilities do we have at our disposal (assets)? Gaps?

What aspects of the situation can we turn to our advantage?

(*continued*)

TOOL 8.5   100-Hour Plan for Crisis Management (continued)

Situational Objectives and Intent

Priority 1: _____ Leader: _____

Actions: _____When: _____Who: _____

Actions: _____When: _____Who: _____

Actions: _____When: _____Who: _____

Priority 2: _____ Leader: _____

Actions: _____When: _____Who: _____

Actions: _____When: _____Who: _____

Actions: _____When: _____Who: _____

Priority 3: _____ Leader: _____

Actions: _____When: _____Who: _____

Actions: _____When: _____Who: _____

Actions: _____When: _____Who: _____

Communication

Primary spokesperson: _____ Backup: _____

Message:

TOOL 8.5   100-Hour Plan for Crisis Management (continued)

Communication points:

1.

2.

3.

Protocols

Next team call/meeting:

Exceptions guidelines:

REFERENCES AND FURTHER READING

Bradt, George, and Bancroft, Ed. 2010. *The Total Onboarding Program: An Integrated Approach to Recruiting, Hiring, and Accelerating Talent Facilitators*. San Francisco: Pfeiffer.

Bradt, George, and Davis, Gillian. 2014. *First-Time Leader: Foundational Tools for Inspiring and Enabling Your New Team*. Hoboken, NJ: John Wiley & Sons.

Bradt, George, and Vonnegut, Mary. 2009. *Onboarding: How to Get Your New Employees Up to Speed in Half the Time*. Hoboken, NJ: John Wiley & Sons.

Bradt, George, 2011–2015. The New Leader's Playbook, articles on www.Forbes.com.

Brown, Brené. 2010. "The Power of Vulnerability." TED Talk video, 20:19. June. http://www.ted.com/talks/brene_brown_on_vulnerability.

Buckingham, Marcus, and Donald Clifton. 2001. *Now, Discover Your Strengths*. New York: Free Press.

Chandran, Rajiv, de la Boutetier, Hortense, and Dewar, Carolyn. 2015. "Ascending to the C-Suite." *McKinsey Insights*, April. www.mckinsey.com/insights/leading_in_the_21st_century/ascending_to_the_c-suite?cid=other-eml-nsl-mip-mck-oth-1505.

Charan, Ram, Drotter, Stephen, and Noel, James. 2001. *The Leadership Pipeline: How to Build the Leadership-Powered Company*. San Francisco: Jossey-Bass.

Covey, Steven. 1989. *The 7 Habits of Highly Effective People*. New York: Simon & Schuster.

Coyne, Kevin, and Edward Coyne. 2007. "Surviving Your New CEO." *Harvard Business Review*, May.

Crabtree, Steve. 2013. "Worldwide, 13% of Employees Are Engaged at Work," *Gallup*, October 8. http://www.gallup.com/poll/165269/worldwide-employees-engaged-work.aspx.

Dattner, Ben. 2011. *The Blame Game: How the Hidden Rules of Credit and Blame Determine Our Success or Failure*. With Darren Dahl. New York: Free Press.

Deutsch, Clay, and Andy West. 2010. Perspectives on Merger Integration. *McKinsey*, June.

Duck, Jeannie Daniel. 2001. *The Change Monster: The Human Forces that Fuel or Foil Corporate Transformation and Change*. New York: Three Rivers Press.

Eliot, T. S. 1943. "Little Gidding." In *Four Quartets*. New York: Harcourt Brace Jovanovich.

Gadiesh, Orit, and James L. Gilbert. 1998. "Profit Pools: A Fresh Look at Strategy." *Harvard Business Review*, May.

Gladwell, Malcolm. 2005. *Blink: The Power of Thinking Without Thinking*. Boston: Little, Brown.

Guber, Peter. 2008. "The Four Truths of the Storyteller." *Harvard Business Review*, January.

Groysberg, Boris, Andrew Hill and Toby Johnson. 2010. "Which of These People Is Your Future CEO? The Different Ways Military Experience Prepares Managers for Leadership," *Harvard Business Review*, November.

Harrald, John R. 2006. "Agility and Discipline: Critical Success Factors for Disaster Response," The Annals of the American Academy of Political and Social Science 604 (March): 256–272.

Hastings, Reed. 2009. "Culture." SlideShare. August 1. http://www.slideshare .net/reed2001/culture-1798664.

Heffernan, Margaret. 2012. "Why Mergers Fail." CBS Money Watch, April 24. http://www.cbsnews.com/news/why-mergers-fail/.

Hilton, Elizabeth. 2001. "Differences in Visual and Auditory Short-Term Memory." *Undergraduate Research Journal* 4. https://www.iusb.edu/ugr-journal/static/2001/hilton.php.

Linver, Sandy. 1983. *Speak and Get Results: The Complete Guide to Speeches and Presentations That Work in Any Business Situation*. With Nick Taylor. New York: Summit.

Maslow, Abraham H. 1943. "A Theory of Human Motivation." *Psychological Review* 50 (4): 370–96.

Masters, Brooke. 2009. "Rise of a Headhunter." *Financial Times*, March 30. www.ft.com/cms/s/0/19975256–1af2-11de-8aa3-0000779fd2ac.html.

Neff, Thomas J., and Citrin, James M. 2005. *You're in Charge, Now What? The 8 Point Plan*. New York: Crown Business.

Neilson, Gary L., Karla L. Martin, and Elizabeth Powers. 2008, "The Secrets to Successful Strategy Execution." *Harvard Business Review*, June, 60.

Schein, Edgar. 1985. *Organizational Culture and Leadership*. San Francisco: Jossey-Bass.

Senge, Peter M. 1990. *The Fifth Discipline: The Art and Practice of the Learning Organization*. New York: Doubleday/Currency.

———. 1994. *The Fifth Discipline Fieldbook: Strategies and Tools for Building a Learning Organization*. Boston: Nicholas Brealey.

Lao-Tzu. 2003. *Tao Te Ching*. Translated by Jonathan Star. New York: Tarcher.

Watkins, Michael. 2003. *The First 90 Days: Critical Success Strategies for New Leaders at All Levels*. Boston: Harvard Business School Press.

George Bradt has led the revolution in how people start new jobs. He progressed through sales, marketing, and general management around the world at companies including Procter & Gamble, Coca-Cola, and J.D. Power's Power Information Network spin-off as chief executive.

Now he is a principal of CEO Connection and chairman of Prime-Genesis, the executive onboarding group he founded in 2002 to accelerate complex transitions for leaders and teams. Since then, George and his partners have reduced new leader failure rates from 40 percent to 5 percent through a single-minded focus on helping them and teams deliver better results faster over their first 100 days.

A graduate of Harvard and Wharton (MBA), George is coauthor of five books on onboarding, a weekly column on Forbes.com, and seven musical plays (book, lyrics, and music). His e-mail address is gbradt@PrimeGenesis.com.

Jayme A. Check offers a dynamic and global perspective on leadership gained from executive roles in firms ranging from start-ups to the Fortune 500 and from Wall Street to Asia. He is recognized for deep expertise in navigating high-growth and rapidly changing environments. Jayme's held leadership positions in sales, business development, and general management at companies including J.P. Morgan, Guidance Solutions, and Brice Manufacturing.

In addition to his active role at PrimeGenesis as a founding partner and author of its executive onboarding methodology, Jayme is CEO of Quantum Global Partners, a firm that provides companies worldwide with results-based leadership development, strategic direction, and senior interim management.

Jayme earned a BS from Syracuse University and an MBA from UCLA's Anderson School. His articles and opinions have appeared in *Bloomberg Businessweek*, Fox Business, and *Talent Management* magazine, among others. Jayme can be reached at jcheck@PrimeGenesis.com.

John Lawler is CEO of PrimeGenesis. Previously he was CEO of three private equity–backed companies, leading business and cultural transformations in a variety of industries. Before that, at LexisNexis, he served as group president and built a new division of high-growth legal technology businesses via acquisition, investment, and integration, and led a successful digital transformation as CEO of Martindale-Hubbell. Earlier, John was an investment banker at Bear Stearns and led transitions and growth initiatives at Dun & Bradstreet.

John is a proven leadership and business consultant, transformational CEO, board member, and coach, with a track record of tapping his experiences to help leaders accelerate growth and superior returns organically and via mergers and acquisitions. He has extensive experience in the Americas, Europe, and Asia. He earned his BA from Williams College and his MBA from the University of Virginia. His e-mail address is jlawler@PrimeGenesis.com.